JC
251
.R4

D1203505

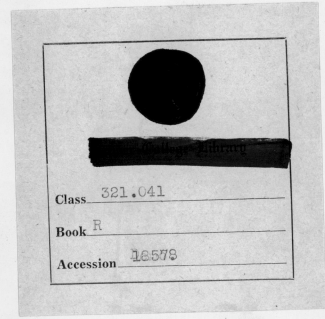

_____ College Library

Class _____ 321.041 _____

Book _____ R _____

Accession _____ 18578 _____

# A Democratic Manifesto

# A Democratic Manifesto

## BY EMERY REVES

### RANDOM HOUSE

*New York*

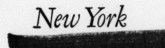

SECOND PRINTING

Copyright, 1942, by Emery Reves

All rights reserved. This book, or parts thereof, cannot
be reproduced without permission of the publishers.

*Published simultaneously in Canada by*
*The Macmillan Company of Canada Limited*

Manufactured in the U. S. A. by H. Wolff, New York

# Contents

Feb. '43

2512

18578

# Dialogue
## between Confucius (*the Master*)
## and Tsze-loo

"1  *Tsze-loo said:* 'The Prince of Wei has been waiting for you in order with you to administer the government. What will you consider the first thing to be done?'

"2  *The Master replied:* 'What is necessary is to rectify names.'

"3  'So, indeed!' *said Tsze-loo.* 'You are wide of the mark. Why must there be such rectification?'

"4  *The Master said:* 'How uncultivated you are! Yew! A superior man, in regard to what he does not know, shows a cautious reserve.'

"5  'If names be not correct, language is not in accordance with the truth of things. If language be not in accordance with the truth of things, affairs cannot be carried on to success.

"6  'When affairs cannot be carried on to success, proprieties and music will not flourish. When proprieties and music do not flourish, punishments will not be properly awarded. When punishments are not properly awarded, the people do not know how to move hand or foot.

"7  'Therefore a superior man considers it necessary that the names he uses may be spoken appropriately, and also that what he speaks may be carried out appropriately. What the superior man requires, is just that in his words there may be nothing incorrect.' "

(CHAPT. III, BOOK XIII, TSZE-LOO of *Confucian Analects*)

# A *Democratic Manifesto*

# I

## *Men or Principles*

TWENTY YEARS after the complete and utter defeat of autocratic and militaristic principles and states, the world is now undergoing the greatest onslaught in history by those same autocratic, militaristic forces. Twenty years after the greatest victory of democratic principles and of democratic nations, democracy is on the defensive all along the line. All the democratic nations of continental Europe have been vanquished and conquered. The two most powerful units of the world—the British Commonwealth of Nations and the United States of America—are forced to mobilize their entire resources in order to defend themselves and to escape defeat and conquest by those very same anti-democratic forces which were laid prostrate by them twenty years ago.

What has happened during those twenty years?

After their victory in 1918, the democratic, freedom-loving nations had full control of and absolute power over this planet. Those forces which were threatening the security and peace of the democracies were not stronger than the few criminals who are always threatening individual security and public order within an organized state.

3

Everybody yearned for peace. Everybody wanted disarmament. Everybody wanted a wider freedom of international
trade. Everybody wanted a better organization of international economic life in order to secure for each nation and
each individual more wealth and greater safety than ever
before. Technical developments seemed to place all those
hopes within the grasp of reality. In spite of the fact that the
forces who supported those aspirations were ten to one—
maybe fifty to one—against those who opposed them, from
1930 onwards, year by year, month by month, we were
steadily marching towards greater armaments, sharper antagonisms, more poverty, diminution of trade, towards intolerance, persecutions, dictatorships, imperialism—towards
the Second World War.

A young man, whose entire education was based on the
hopes of the nineteen-twenties, and who followed closely
step by step those events which led to the Second World
War, can hardly understand this baffling development, unless he had been completely misled by the disintegrating
propaganda of a movement of demagogic masses. Ponder
as he will, there seems nothing for him to do but admit that
he understands nothing in this world, and to think back to
the words he learned at school—the words uttered by the
Swedish Chancellor Oxenstierna, when he sent his son in
1648 as Minister Plenipotentiary to Westphalia: "You will
see, my son, with what little wisdom this world is governed." He must ask himself fearfully: *Where* is even this
iota of wisdom with which the world is supposed to be
governed?

The simplest way to explain this rapid and almost catastrophic decline of the democracies during the short period between 1920 and 1940 is to accuse certain statesmen who have committed the greatest blunders. We like to blame the inefficiency of the liberal regimes of Nitti and Facta for the advent of Mussolini, and the weaknesses of the Weimar Republic for the advent of Hitler. We used to blame Lodge, Borah, Reed and the other isolationist Senators for the torpedoing of the League of Nations, even before it was launched. We used to condemn Clemenceau, Poincaré and the other French nationalists for having prevented the strengthening of democracy in Germany. We hold Sir Austen Chamberlain and the Tories in England responsible for the failure of the Geneva Protocol. We believe MacDonald, Baldwin and Henderson are the men responsible for British disarmament and weakness. We think that Pilsudski and Beck are to be blamed for the failure of an Eastern Locarno. We have accused Sir Samuel Hoare and Pierre Laval for the betrayal of Ethiopia and the sabotaging of the League. We think that Neville Chamberlain, Daladier and Georges Bonnet are the men who committed the crime of Munich. We used to accuse Leon Blum and Pierre Cot of being responsible for the weaknesses of the French armed forces. And we used to accuse Charles Lindbergh, Senator Wheeler, Nye, Johnson and others for American isolationism and for having made it impossible for the United States to be adequately prepared to meet attack.

All these personal responsibilities are valid, but only to a certain degree. They cannot explain the iron logic of the events which have taken place in this strange period between the two world wars. They cannot offer explanations because obviously none of these statesmen was able to control events or to lead his country. They were controlled and led by greater forces. Several examples prove that. When public opinion in England and France revolted against the policy of Hoare and Laval in the Ethiopian conflict, their strongest opponents, Anthony Eden and Yvon Delbos replaced them. Shortly after the Ethiopian incident, another conflict of the same forces arose—the Spanish "Civil War." And in this conflict, carrying the most powerfully felt international repercussions, Eden and Delbos committed exactly the same errors for which they so vehemently denounced their predecessors, and handled this new problem in exactly the same way as Hoare and Laval would have handled it. Innumerable citations of this kind could be made.

It is indisputable that the human quality of the leaders of democracy between the two wars was not on a par with those of their predecessors of the nineteenth century. If any private enterprise were managed in the way that the great democratic nations have been managed during the past years, certainly the directors of that enterprise would be discharged.

It seems to be a law in the history of great nations or great families that after a certain time a generation arises which lacks those qualities which are indispensable for effective leadership and continued progress. This is usually the time when such families and such nations suffer decline. It is a tragic symptom which arises periodically and which can only be overcome by an infusion of fresh blood.

However weak the statesmen of the democratic nations

may have been, they have not been altogether the criminals and imbeciles that public imagination believes when judging them by all those blunders which are identified with their names. The long series of defeats, the gradual sinking from world domination to subjugation certainly can not be adequately explained by the lack of statesmanship of our leaders, no matter to what extent they have been responsible.

Another school of thought will make us believe that this reversal of the tide in human history was caused by the great dynamic forces represented by the Nazi, Fascist and other totalitarian movements all over the world. They say that Hitler and Mussolini are tyrants, megalomaniacs, militarists, ruthless demagogues, and that they and their gangs are responsible for the ills and miseries of the world.

However obvious and simple such an explanation may appear to be, it cannot stand close examination.

The democracies were overwhelmingly powerful when these movements were started a few years ago by a limited number of individuals. These movements could have been stopped and destroyed on innumerable occasions, with a minimum of effort, energy and force. No democracy was able or willing to do so, although these anti-democratic forces never made any attempt to conceal their character, their programs and their purpose.

To accuse the Nazis or the Fascists of sole responsibility for this war is like accusing the tuberculosis microbe of causing tuberculosis.

Of course, it does. It is its only and inevitable object.

For many years we were aware of what the virus of Fascism was doing in the blood stream of a nation, just as we know what the microbe of tuberculosis does from the moment it begins to develop in the lung of a man. But if a man infected with tuberculosis refuses to fight it, flagrantly and willfully ignores the advice of his doctor and allows his entire organism to be ravished by the microbe, then it cannot be said that his death was caused by the microbe. His death was caused rather by his own lack of will and capacity to fight that microbe.

Years ago the Nazis and Fascists declared that they wanted to destroy the democratic way of life, the Christian religion, and every form of individual liberty. They condemned peace and pacifism and declared war to be the natural way of life.

They educated their youth on a strictly militaristic basis. They wanted to prepare for and wage wars of conquest, believing it to be a historical law that the strong nations should conquer and rule the weaker ones.

In view of the fact that this program was openly promulgated for years, that it was repeated in speeches and writings, that it was openly and rapidly put into operation, it is impossible to declare in the midst of this world struggle that the responsibility lies only with Hitler. He was a ridiculous, miserable, ineffectual nobody when he first proclaimed his program, but the great democracies permitted him to grow stronger and stronger until he became so powerful as to challenge the whole human race.

No, Hitler cannot be looked upon as solely responsible for this world catastrophe. He is following his vocation. He is the incarnation of evil that Providence brings forth from time to time in order to remind man that peace, liberty, happiness, tolerance, fraternity, progress, man's rights, nay, even the right to exist, are not natural endowments, but the fruits of centuries of tremendous struggle, surpassed only by the struggle necessary to maintain and keep this heritage.

Almost every day we listen to orators or we read articles and books by commentators and political writers, deploring the long series of failures committed by the democracies during the past years. These critics say: If only Sir John Simon had taken a stand against the Japanese in Manchuria . . . If only Britain and France had applied sanctions against Italy to stop her aggression in Ethiopia . . . If only the Popular Front Government in France had sufficiently supported the Republicans in Spain . . . If only this or that nation, if only this or that statesman had done this or that . . .

All this is obviously correct. It is certain that if the democratic powers had been willing to sacrifice 5,000 soldiers in Manchuria, 10,000 soldiers in order to save Ethiopia, 20,000 soldiers to prevent the Germans and Italians from establishing a puppet regime in Spain, if they had been prepared to risk 50,000 soldiers to prevent the occupation of Austria, it would not have been necessary two or three years later for the British Empire and the United States to mobilize their entire man power, from 18 to 65, and to spend a hundred billion dollars or more a year for armaments.

But in spite of these "if only's . . .", in spite of these many conditional arguments, it remains a fact that no democracy ever was in a position or willing to take the step that might have averted the catastrophe. Why?

In many cases, it was possible for the democratic powers

to act efficiently at the right moment, but none of them did. Why?

In the reply to this question, in the proper diagnosis of the past twenty years lies the only hope of a better future. It is obvious that the real cause of the disaster and of the impossibility to stop it must lie deeper than merely in the failure of certain individuals or certain governments.

In our anger and helpless fury we call Hitler and his associates "criminals," "outlaws," "gangsters." But have we the right to use such big words?

What is a "criminal"?

There is no other possible definition of a criminal than that he is a man who violates some existing law accepted by the community.

But where were the laws Hitler supposedly violated? Were we ever prepared to enact international legislation, so that its terms would be binding and its violation could have been called a crime? Such laws have never existed and the great democracies have refused to enact them when they had an opportunity to organize a new world. They refused to accept any international order other than the old one created by agreements and treaties between sovereign nations. Such agreements and treaties cannot be regarded as laws unless one of the parties is prepared to apply force if the other party violates them.

But has any one of the democracies been willing to punish Germany or Italy or Japan when they violated those primitive laws which are made by international treaties? Whenever such a treaty was unilaterally violated, the law-abiding democracies always accepted the *fait accompli*. And from a purely moral point of view, it is difficult to say what is a greater crime—to violate a law or to tolerate such violation.

In every sphere of life—in private life, in family life, in business life—the only recognized correct way to conduct affairs is by a course of thought-out, well-planned action which goes beyond merely the possible advantages, benefits and comforts of the next five minutes following the action. Every private individual, every businessman, the head of every family has to conduct his affairs in such a way that any event that might happen tomorrow or the following day will not catch him unawares, unprepared and completely at a loss.

Only in public life is it required that statesmen and governments need not go beyond consideration of the immediate problems of the present. They are required to restrict their thoughts and activities to the most urgent and unavoidable questions of the day, whether or not such *ad hoc* solutions of immediate problems are advantageous or disadvantageous to the nation, seen not only from the point of view of the day of action, but in a perspective of a few years, or even just a few months.

In every other field of life we call such conduct of affairs careless and frivolous. In politics, we call it "realistic."

In every field of life, the method of conducting affairs which looks beyond the events that might happen in later years, we call wise and far-sighted. In public affairs, we call it "unrealistic" and "Utopian."

The democracies have been driven by their enemies and by their confused leaders to the acceptance of that sophism which seeks to persuade us that a realistic policy is not a policy which creates realities, but a policy which at any given moment bows before the realities created by the others.

The total chaos in which the entire human race has been plunged today, is the result of the complete disruption of all the moral and spiritual values which history has developed. After many thousands of years of religious, moral, social and political progress we find ourselves once again in a world as strange, as insecure, as unexplored as Adam must have found it after his expulsion from the Garden of Eden.

There is no other way out of this confusion, except to start again at the very beginning. We must undertake a thorough examination of all those elementary principles on which our social and political life is built. There are some twenty of these elementary, basic notions, the meaning of which has been so completely confused that nobody knows any more what their exact import is, how they react, in what form they can be applied and how they must be handled. We must start where Confucius said all statesmanship must start: To give the words we are using their exact and unmistakable meaning.

If we analyze these elementary principles of a democratic order, we shall see that the interpretation given to them by our existing constitutions, laws, rules and customs are utterly inadequate, that in most cases they are in total contradiction to the very essence of these principles themselves, and that we let ideals which have always been the most powerful propelling force of human progress and advancement degenerate into meaningless words devoid of any substance.

We shall see that the "democratic order" we want to defend is no more a democratic order at all—merely *the first attempt* towards it, undertaken at the end of the eighteenth century and based on conditions and considerations of the eighteenth century.

The complete lack of any reaction to the Atlantic Charter, the complete lack of enthusiasm with which it has been received in the democratic countries, prove that the peoples have an unconscious feeling of the unreality of this past order.

An examination of the real meaning of these basic principles of social and international life, will reveal that there is no democratic order to defend, but that there *is* a democratic world order *to create*.

The correct interpretation of these principles, the understanding of their reactions upon each other, give us the only proper diagnosis of the decadence of that order which was established in 1919, and which was supposed to be the basis of a world "safe for democracy." Such a diagnosis of the causes of the present chaos in itself consists of 90 per cent of the therapeutic measures which are needed to organize a democratic world founded on the economic, social and political realities as they present themselves in the middle of the twentieth century.

# II

# *Freedom*

THE GREAT motor of human history is the struggle for freedom. Practically all wars were fought for freedom. All revolutions were launched for freedom. All human endeavors in the scientific, economic and technical fields take their impulse from the desire for greater freedom. The idea of freedom is the origin of practically all the ideals in the political and social fields for which men are fighting today, just as they fought for thousands of years. And yet no notion has created greater confusion than the idea of freedom.

What freedom really is, we still do not know, and it is wide open to interpretation. These various interpretations of the idea "freedom" are the cause of that inextricable confusion in which the various nations, the various ideologies, the various parties and various classes are bitterly opposed to each other. However difficult it appears, we must try to define as clearly as possible what freedom is, if we want to operate with this idea so that we may approach it and not destroy it.

Unfortunately, we are used to debate about political, social and religious principles by the dialectical method. We

14

have not yet available a better, more abstract and more scientific method of research and debate.

This dialectical method, which we find already very highly developed in the works of the Greek philosophers, is operating with contrasts, with antitheses. We say that freedom is the antithesis of compulsion, that peace is the antithesis of war, that independence is the antithesis of commitment, and so on. In order to understand how dangerous it is to follow this road, we must remember that this dialectical method of philosophy, after its highest expression in the dialogues of Plato, led straight ahead to the Sophistic school.

If we examine all these notions on which each controversy on political and social problems is based, we can easily see that what we regard as opposing conceptions are in fact on the same level and express identical phenomena in different degrees.

Liberty without equality is an inconceivable state of affairs. As equality between men, nations or between any other human groupings is obviously against nature—it never existed and probably never will exist—freedom in its pure and total conception would result in a state of affairs which would be the exact opposite of any kind of freedom.

If we gave every man—strong and weak—and every nation—large and small—complete freedom of action without imposing any restriction whatsoever on their impulses, it would result in the greatest terror, oppression, violence—in total anarchy.

It is obvious, therefore, that that kind of freedom which we regard as a human ideal is some kind of a synthesis between freedom and compulsion. The fact that some outside power forbids me to kill a man I dislike, or to take away the property of those who have more than I, considerably restrains my freedom. But this very same restraint protects me from being murdered by those who dislike me, and of being robbed by those who envy whatever I may possess. I definitely have the feeling that being protected against assassination and theft *adds* to my feeling of liberty in greater proportion to how much this same restriction *deprives* me of my liberty in prohibiting me from committing these same acts against others.

This very simple and obvious inter-relationship could be illustrated by any number of examples. But no matter how many examples we may cite, it appears evident that freedom and compulsion have a functional relationship and cannot be regarded as contrasts. The ideal of freedom, as we conceive it, is, therefore, an entirely relative notion depending upon two factors: first, to what degree man can act freely; and second, to what degree he is exposed to the free actions of others. It is only in the right synthesis of these two factors that the optimum can be achieved and that we can bring about a state of affairs among men which might be called freedom.

This close inter-relationship between freedom and compulsion in the social life among men has been recognized at the very beginning of our civilization. The most primitive forms of social life began with the prohibition of certain acts. The fundaments of the Christian religion are the Ten Commandments, stating clearly ten acts which "Thou shalt . . ." or "Thou shalt not . . ."

We may, therefore, state, however paradoxical it may sound, that freedom in the history of mankind started with the first legal imposition of a compulsion.

These original and age-old compulsions were limited to those most primitive impulses of men, the prohibition of which obviously means more freedom for the community than its free exercise.

From the Ten Commandments to the most intricate legislation of our days, there is one clear line: Only through legal restrictions of the free exercise of human impulses can we achieve a state of affairs which we may call "freedom."

In social life this is self-evident, and nobody except an anarchist would pretend that the laws prohibiting assassination, theft, perjury, forgery or overdraft of a bank account are laws contrary to the principle of freedom. We all know that, with the progress of civilization, our social life is becoming more and more complicated, and that this evolution demands more and more compulsion on human actions, and that only the total of these compulsions can give us freedom.

It is of the utmost importance to understand clearly the inter-relationship between freedom and compulsion if we want to solve all those many political, economic and international problems with which we are confronted.

The peculiar thing is that this inter-relationship between freedom and compulsion which is an age-old experience in our social life and which has been all through our history the basic principle of the great legislators and the founders of religion, in order to put some system into the social relationship between man and man, and create the maximum possible individual freedom, has not yet been accepted nor recognized as a basic principle in the political field and in international relations among nations.

In these two important fields in which the present crisis is raging, we still maintain that freedom and compulsion are contradictory, that any compulsion is against the principle of freedom, and that established freedoms can only be maintained without any compulsion. Hence the anarchic situation in which we are living.

The democratic countries have established as a great historic achievement freedom of speech, freedom of the press, freedom of assembly and many other political freedoms, to be enjoyed equally by all citizens. These freedoms have been granted without any limitations and without any clear definition, without any restriction, with the result that in most countries freedom of speech, freedom of the press, freedom of assembly and all the other freedoms have been destroyed only and solely because these freedoms have been granted in an absolute form, in the belief that any restriction or compulsion would be contradictory to the principles of the freedoms granted.

The fact that in so many countries in our generation these freedoms, so dearly paid for through centuries of fighting for them, have been destroyed only and entirely by the freedom of actions these democratic privileges granted to the enemies of freedom, is sufficient proof that as established in their absolute form these freedoms do not guarantee freedom.

It makes no sense that a free and democratic country should give to everybody unlimited freedom and every democratic means to combat freedom and democracy itself. The doctrinaire democrats believe that such a condition is inherent in the principles of democracy and it is against these so-called, but never defined, democratic principles to grant freedoms in varying degrees to different people. This is a very simple and self-evident viewpoint, if we operate with the notion that freedom and compulsion are in contrast. But such a way of thinking is fundamentally erroneous. In the public life of a nation the relationship between freedom and compulsion is exactly the same as in social life, and whether or not we shall enjoy political freedom will depend entirely on the right interpretation of these principles.

The problems concerning the international relationship of peoples are exactly of the same character. Based on the absolute conception of freedom, we arrived at the conceptions of national independence and national sovereignty as the highest expressions of the freedom of a state in its relationship to other states. We believe that any limitation of these absolute conceptions of sovereignty and independence would be contrary to the ideal of freedom of a nation. It is thanks to this conception of absolute freedom, which has created in the international field the same anarchic situation as absolute freedom would create in the social life of any community, that so many nations have been attacked, defeated and conquered, with brute force as the only arbiter among nations, and that hundreds of millions of people have become slaves again.

# III

# *Liberalism*

THE POLITICAL thought that tried to put into reality in the social life the ideals of freedom was Liberalism. Liberal ideas have been the nucleus of programs which attracted the most influential forces at the end of the eighteenth century simultaneously in the United States, in England and in France. The Constitution of the United States, the French Revolution and the beginning of modern industrialism in England gave a tremendous impetus to these ideas and the progressive elements of all the democratic countries were gathered into political parties, the purpose of which was to organize the state and the economic life on the basis of individual liberty, to safeguard the independence of the nations and to create the widest possible freedom of international exchange.

Today the liberal parties are everywhere on the decline, their influence vanishing and their power waning.

The defeat of the liberal parties is a most extraordinary phenomenon. There are two reasons for this. The first one, rather paradoxical, is the acceptance of the liberal-democratic principles by almost all the other political parties in the democracies. In England, both the Conservative Party and the Labor Party became "liberal." By this development they have taken away the main arguments of the Liberal Party. The same evolution can be observed also in all the other democratic countries. Both the Democratic and the Republican Parties in the United States are "liberal."

The second reason for the decline of the liberal parties is the equally paradoxical fact that they became automatically anti-liberal by developing into more and more doctrinaire parties with concrete and rigid programs which they defended with the most a-liberal fanaticism. This reactionary tendency of the liberal and radical bourgeois forces is in total contradiction to the original ideas of liberalism aiming at a political and social liberation of the individual in order to open to every man and every nation a free road to evolution.

If we examine the political thoughts and parties of the democratic countries, whether a country has only two or three parties, or twenty or thirty different parties, we can divide all these apparently divergent programs and parties into two groups in which we can include all the existing and conceivable political thoughts.

In the first group we can place all those parties, movements and groups which believe in a tangible, clearly-worked out program. From this point of view, the revolutionary and the reactionary parties belong in the very same group. There is no difference whatsoever between them from a political or theoretical standpoint, except the element of time. The program of our present-day conservative parties was revolutionary two hundred years ago, and the program of our present-day revolutionaries, if they achieve it, will be reactionary one hundred years hence. Those principles and programs which are today fervently defended by the Republican Party in the United States, the Conservatives in England, and the right-wing bourgeois circles in France, were looked upon as revolutionary before the American and French Revolutions, and their defenders were regarded as dangerous elements in the state, many of them being executed as such.

On the other hand, the Communist Party and the Communist program, which we regard as the most revolutionary forces of our time, become conservative as soon as they are established. Whatever our opinion about Communism may be, the regime of the Bolshevik Party in Russia is the prototype of a conservative regime. They adhere most fanatically to a concrete and established system, defending it by every means. They do not tolerate any opposing view and whoever openly tries to change anything in the existing established order meets with the same fate as the liberals met under absolutism, and the fate which the Communists, themselves, meet in many democratic-capitalistic countries.

In the second category, we can group all such parties and political movements which do not believe in the perfection of any closed system and detailed program whether already existing or to be created, but which believe in constant progress, in the necessity of constant changes in the social, political and economic institutions in order to adapt them to the realities at each given time. Those adhering to this belief were the various liberal and radical parties at their inception.

History proves that this second political conception is nearer to reality, as we cannot trace back in the past any political or social system which was realized in its pure and integral form, nor can we discover any period in which changes would not have taken place.

According to the principles of liberalism, there should be freedom of speech, freedom of assembly, freedom of the press, freedom of voting, the right to elect representatives. These freedoms have been granted to all, and Voltaire's famous words—"I wholly disapprove of what you say and will defend to the death your right to say it"—were self-evident.

Such a state of affairs, granting every individual complete freedom of speech, freedom of the press, freedom of assembly, and granting every association and party complete freedom of activity and of representation in parliament, is the logical result of the triumph of the ideals of the French and American Revolutions and of British reforms.

Unfortunately, this conception left out only one element —the element of Man. Its theories and institutions were based on the abstraction of a "homo democraticus" just as the liberal school of economic thought was based on the abstraction of a "homo economicus." These abstractions worked quite well in theory and in practice so long as the great masses of the new liberal democratic order felt only the advantages of the new era in contrast to the *ancien régime,* which was still vivid in their memories.

But as soon as the economic and political evolutions created one crisis after another, one major war after another; as soon as it was realized that the liberal democratic systems as established could not solve the problem of distribution and could solve only partially the problem of production;

as soon as it became evident that the rise in living standards following the establishment of the liberal democratic regime was not constant; as soon as the political and nationalistic forces intervened in the free exchange of goods and migration, entire classes and nations saw no further chances of amelioration within the existing system. As soon as the masses became conscious of these problems, the elements "homo economicus" and "homo democraticus" did not react in the same way as their creators intended them to.

Dogmatic liberalism, which has permeated all the major political parties, all the governments, the entire civil service and the entire diplomatic corps of the democratic powers, was totally unable to cope with the new situation. Dissatisfied elements began to attack publicly the democratic order. Nothing was done against them because the existing democratic order guaranteed to every citizen "freedom of speech."

More and more people, dissatisfied with the existing order, gathered together and began to organize and to hold meetings against the established principles of democracy. No steps were taken to curb them, because the laws in force guaranteed "freedom of assembly."

Embittered and disillusioned intellectuals, soldiers, bankers and industrialists who never liked the form of popular government, joined the oppositional groups, supported them financially and socially, and soon we saw books, pamphlets, magazines and newspapers published and distributed with the sole purpose of fighting the existing democratic order. No measures were taken against them because they were working on a strictly legal basis which guaranteed them "freedom of the press."

The movement grew more and more powerful, taking the form of political parties which achieved election into parliaments. In every legislative assembly representatives appeared in ever-growing numbers with the sole purpose of fighting in the parliaments against the institution of parliamentarism. Nothing was done against them because their actions were guaranteed by constitutional rights.

Thus the liberal democratic states were undermined, their public life poisoned, and their institutions finally destroyed, by entirely "legal" methods, first in Italy, then in Germany, then in one country after another—spreading like wildfire.

A passionate controversy arose between the real believers in the democratic principles and those ruling circles who were constantly retreating and who had given up one democratic position after another before the ruthlessly attacking enemy. The argument was always the same: We are a democracy; our citizens have constitutionally guaranteed rights, and we cannot act against them in an anti-democratic way.

So they withdrew. And when they found themselves faced with the alternative, to capitulate or change their methods, their dogmatism was so deeply rooted, that they preferred to capitulate.

The disastrous consequences of liberal democratic dogmatism lie open before everybody's eyes. The tragedy is that the liberal leaders were so blinded by their theoretical dogmatism that they refused to understand the present-day problems, even after they lost most of the major battles, and they defended the last ditch of their abstract conceptions with a conviction worthy of a better cause.

Innumerable are the public utterances of the defeated liberal leaders trying to justify their positions in the battle. Their unchangeable views were best expressed in a single phrase written by the leader of the English liberals, Lord Samuel, in an essay published in *The Nineteenth Century and After,* as late as June, 1938. Lord Samuel argued against those who urged a change of methods in our relationship with dictatorial powers, saying: "To be liberal only towards liberal states is not liberalism at all."

This one phrase expresses the unreality of dogmatic liberalism which is mostly responsible for the paralyzing of our governments, our diplomats and our civil servants.

If we try to analyze these democratic principles, it appears to be the most simple logic that in organized society liberty of speech cannot signify liberty of speech for those who want to abolish liberty of speech.

Freedom of the press cannot mean freedom of the press for such publications which seek to suppress freedom of the press.

Freedom of vote cannot mean freedom of vote for those who want to abolish freedom of vote.

The tribunal of parliaments has not been created for those who want to destroy parliamentarism.

The democratic institutions have not been created for and cannot be at the disposal of those who want to abolish democracy.

These simple deductions appear to be self-evident and almost axiomatic in debating the principles of democracy.

But if there are certain people who do not want to accept the results of logical thinking, they should read and re-read the history of the past twenty years of all the democratic countries. They will have to realize that democracy was destroyed everywhere by means granted to their conquerors by the democracies themselves. In this world of reality, every system, every nation has to perish if it has nothing but pious sermons of non-violence with which to oppose cruel forces.

The victory of the totalitarian dictatorships and the defeat of the democratic institutions do not mean at all the defeat of democratic principles, but they do mean the total defeat of that peculiar interpretation of democratic principles on which we have based our existence during the past decades.

We thought it was sufficient to proclaim certain rules among liberally and democratically minded people in order to live in a democracy, something like an exclusive club where we may live among gentlemen, respecting the rules and regulations of the club.

But our exclusive social order was overthrown by a great number of newcomers whose only purpose in joining the club was to loot the kitchen and to cheat at the poker tables.

If we want to establish a democratic order, not in a vacuum and not based on the abstraction of a "homo democraticus," then we cannot proceed by presupposing that the most important element in our construction—the element, Man—will react in any manner other than it has to according to its qualities and natural conditions.

Democracy, like every high form of culture and civilization, is to a certain degree a luxury which can only be understood and appreciated by men of a certain education, and which can only be established after the satisfaction of certain more primitive needs. As it is inconceivable that in our time all human beings will have the understanding, the knowledge, the vision, the character and the moral capacity to act and react as democratic men have to act and react, we can only make democracy work if we are prepared to create the necessary defenses for a democratic regime, enacting and promulgating in an unmistakable form what we understand under each one of the freedoms granted by the regime, and if we establish simultaneously with the granting of these freedoms, the required institutions for their defense and for the prevention of their destruction.

The basic principle of a correct interpretation of liberal democratic institutions is that democratic institutions are created for all those who are democratically minded, and the only possible interpretation of liberal policy is that each individual, each party and each nation must be treated according to their own principles.

This is the only possible interpretation which would allow us to reorganize a democratic world order so that democratic peoples attached to democratic institutions would be free from attack and destruction from within their own nations or from outside forces.

Freedom of speech means that every individual has the right to express his thoughts and to have complete freedom to say whatever he wants to say, with one single exception: He shall have no right to say that he is against freedom of speech.

Freedom of the press means that every individual has the right to print books, periodicals or newspapers and to publish in such printed media any idea he wishes, with one exception: He shall have no right to print or publish that freedom of the press is an institution which is bad and which must be abolished.

All individuals must have freedom of assembly and in such assemblies every individual must have the liberty to express whatever views he may hold, with one single exception: He shall have no right to attack or to criticize the right of free assembly.

Every political party must have the right to be admitted to legislative assemblies, and every duly elected representative must have the right to express freely his views on public affairs, with one single exception: No speaker shall have the right to attack the institution of parliamentarism and representative government, and no parties advocating such views shall be permitted to participate in parliamentary debates.

The last aim of democracy is naturally the democratic man, but in view of the fact that the human race, even the most highly civilized nations, are not comprised entirely of democratic men, we must secure democracy for those who are democratically minded and it is our primary democratic duty to oppose anti-democratic thoughts, movements and forces with anti-democratic methods.

We realized a long time ago that the only way to guarantee the safety of the lives of peaceful citizens is to have an organization which segregates those individuals who interfere with the peaceful lives of others. And we know equally well that the only way to guarantee the safety of the personal property of citizens is to have an organization to deprive those individuals of their personal properties, who interfere with the personal properties of others.

There is no possibility of a workable democracy either on a national or on an international scope without safeguarding the political rights of the democratic people by such coercive institutions which would prevent and restrict the activities of those elements which for any reason are working against the democratic privileges of democratic citizens or nations.

Only if we define quite clearly what we understand under each one of the democratic freedoms which our states can grant to the individuals, and only if we establish the necessary organism for the prevention and the suppression of all such forces which are working against those democratic privileges, and only if we accept the doctrines that liberal policy means to be liberal towards those who are liberally minded and to treat all individuals, parties or nations according to their own principles, can we hope that in future we shall be able to stop at any time such movements as are represented in our generation by Nazism and Fascism. Only then can we hope that we shall have a democratic order that will work according to the present realities of our world.

# IV

# *Nation*

With National Socialism a new conception came into power which is in absolute contradiction to the ideas upon which international life has hitherto been based by all states, democratic or autocratic. A very serious examination of this new conception is necessary in order to avoid the final destruction of a democratic world order and in order to be able to pursue a realistic policy and stop making politics in a vacuum.

This destructive conception, which has had such a devastating effect in the course of a few years, is the National Socialist theory about the "Nation." To know exactly what we mean when we speak about "Nation" is of the greatest importance, as this is the starting point of all political action in the relationship between peoples.

According to the democratic thesis, accepted by all the Western countries and unchallenged during the past century, Nation is the totality of the population composed of all races, believing in all religions, speaking all languages, united by the same ideal in the same state.

National Socialism has replaced this theory by another

one, according to which the "Nation" (*Volk*) is the totality of a people of the same race, of the same language, of the same origin—*"Volkstum"*—independently of the state or states in which they reside.

These two conceptions are fundamentally opposed to each other.

The democratic conception clearly defines the units of international life and permits the development of a policy the basis of which is fixed. These units are the formations: States. According to this theory, the nations, "Great Britain," "Germany," "United States of America," "France," "Brazil," are clearly defined. All international acts, conventions, treaties, alliances, the organization of the relationship among the different peoples can be based on well-founded components.

The Nazi theory entirely reverses this established order. The "Reich" is, of course, a state as before and like the others, but it is not identical with the juridical form of the "German Nation." Naturally, a Prussian or a Bavarian is a German as before, but according to this theory, Rumanians in Transylvania, Americans in Minnesota, and Brazilians in Sao Paulo, if they are of German descent and origin, belong equally to the "German Nation," must owe allegiance to the German Reich and must be in the services of the German Government.

According to this theory, a nation is a physical and psychological construction and essentially a racial and cultural community, and not a politico-territorial construction. The German Nation, therefore, is not conditional to the German

State, as "Nation" and "State" are two entirely independent conceptions.

Hitler says in *Mein Kampf* that the German Reich as a state embraces all Germans, not only in order to maintain racial elements of this nation everywhere, but also to raise the German Nation to a dominating position all over the world. The German Minister of Interior Frick, in a pamphlet designed for Germans residing overseas, says that every American of German blood must always remember wherever he may find himself that he is a part of Germany. And the Nazi theoretician Alfred Rosenberg, in his *Myth of the Twentieth Century,* declares that "the infamous conception of the state of the nineteenth century must be crushed."

Naturally, scientists, statesmen and public opinion in democratic countries rejected this National Socialistic doctrine about the Nation, but they rejected it with a benign smile and with that conceited self-assurance which is so characteristic of our generation. The democratic nations did not want to take seriously these "unreasonable" views and did not believe that they were in any way menacing their institutions and their existence. And when these theories were put into practice in Germany, they thought that this was a German internal affair which could not in any way affect the internal life and policies of the democratic peoples. They also firmly believed that Germany and the other totalitarian powers with their conceptions of the "Nation" could well exist and live side by side with the democratic countries with their democratic-juridical conception of the "Nation."

In reality, this was identical with allowing wolves and sheep to live in the same fold. The acceptance of the Nazi conception of the Nation permitted the Nazi Government the untrammeled organization of racially Germanic citizens in Denmark and Brazil, in Yugoslavia and Chile, in France and the United States, and in practically all countries in the world. This organization meant not merely the maintenance of cultural bonds with the Fatherland. It meant the education of these foreign citizens of German descent in a National Socialistic and anti-democratic sense; the training of them in military formations; the drilling of them in espionage and sabotage work, inculcating ideas in them and fostering attitudes hostile to the states in which they were living; the turning of them into military shock troops against the countries of which they were, in a democratic sense, the Nationals.

This undermining of the democratic nations became so strong that it was one of the main weapons of the totalitarian powers in their world war of conquest against the democracies, and in many cases it was sufficient to prepare the victim countries for military occupation without any noticeable resistance. The democratic powers were entirely helpless and unable to defend themselves against this devastatingly powerful political-warfare machine which the National Socialist Government, based on the racial conception of the Nation, built up during several years quite openly and visibly.

To prevent an American or a French citizen from saying and writing what he thought was against the constitutional guarantee of free speech, and according to the existing dem-

ocratic principles, it was impossible to differentiate between
loyal democratic citizens and such citizens who were obviously the enemies of the state and the agents of the anti-
democratic powers. The democratic governments were able
to differentiate only between "citizens" and "aliens," as they
were defined according to the existing democratic laws,
however inadequate and insufficient they apparently were.
Nothing was done in this respect in the democratic countries until it was too late, and then in desperate moments,
the only thing that was done was the rounding up of
"aliens," most of them the most passionate fighters for
democracy, and the first victims of the Nazi political conceptions.

Nothing could be done concerning those many thousands
of Danish, American, Yugoslav or French "citizens," who
with all their power worked and fought for the destruction
of the country of which juridically they were citizens, and
for the victory of Nazi Germany in whose service—con-
sciously or unconsciously—they were. If a small number of
these "citizens" was arrested, it was due to the fact that in
one way or another it was possible to build up cases based on
accusations against them which were different from their
real crimes.

It is a foregone conclusion that this state of affairs,
wherein a democratic state can be undermined and destroyed from within by its own citizens entirely through the
present interpretation of the democratic conception of the
Nation, is intolerable, and self-contradictory. We must set a
clear and unequivocal definition of the notions of "Nation"

and "National," if we want to prevent the total destruction of democratic institutions everywhere.

The democratic conception of the Nation is the only political corollary of Christian principles. According to Christian principles, every man is made in the image of God and is equal in the eyes of God if he accepts the symbols of Christianity and the authority of the Church. It, therefore, must be regarded as an axiom of organized democracy that all citizens must be equal, provided they abide by the laws of their country and accept the authority of democratic constitution. It is a revolting creed that men should be debased to animal breeding and be classified according to color of hair, number of teeth, or the origin of their grandmothers.

But the democratic conception of the Nation, which endows each citizen with equality and the right to enjoy all the privileges of that status, can only be for such individuals who on their part accept this democratic conception and the authority of the laws expressing this conception. There is no place in a democratic state for any individual who is not 100 per cent loyal to these democratic conceptions. To repudiate them, to preach racial theories, or any other views opposing the democratic conception of the Nation, to be in any way in the service of foreign governments, championing Nazi-Fascist principles, must be regarded as crimes of the most serious nature, punishable in peace time as rigorously as are acts of treason in times of war.

The democratic conception of the Nation must be clearly interpreted and such interpretation must be expressed through legislation which would assure a free and democratic way of life to all those who believe in a free and democratic way of life, but which would impose severe penalties on all those who use freedom and democracy as their tools with which to destroy the free and democratic way of life.

Without such a new interpretation and legislation, the democratic nations are entirely at the mercy of their enemies—the Fascist totalitarian states—who under present conditions have all the facilities with which to destroy democracy from the inside. Restriction of immigration, or control over aliens, is a very naive attempt to ward off this danger. All the leading fifth columnists and traitors, all those who really had power to help the Nazi and Japanese conquests, were Nationals of their own countries. The German, Italian or Spanish political refugees were at the last moment put into concentration camps, but Laval, Baudouin, De Brinon, Quisling, Mussert, Tiso, as well as thousands of their henchmen, were looked upon as patriots, until they were able to give the final blow to the free institutions of their own peoples.

It is imperative for those few countries who still enjoy democracy to become fully aware of the realities of the crisis, and to understand that Laval and Quisling and Antonescu are not in power because they were criminals and traitors, but because the existing laws of their respective countries, as long as they were democracies, did not provide the legal means to the democratic governments to prevent their subversive anti-democratic acts and actions, and gave them full liberty to destroy liberty.

# V

# *Nationalism*

THE GREAT CRISIS which has been ravaging the world since the beginning of the twentieth century, which had broken out on a large scale in 1914, and the third phase of which we are now traversing, has not yet been explained clearly enough. A great many economic, political, financial, technical and moral explanations have been offered by various thinkers and writers. All of them are right from their particular points of view, but they all refer only to a partial phenomenon and do not give an indication of the real origin of this world catastrophe, which, in spite of the complexity of its effects, is not very difficult to reveal.

During the past 150 years, two powerful streams have engulfed the human race and have dragged it into different directions with irresistible force.

One of these streams is the industrial evolution. The enormous development of industry, which started at the beginning of the nineteenth century and was destined to raise the material welfare of humanity to a level undreamed of up to then, has for its fundamental and ruling character an imperious tendency towards *universalism*. The quickened rhythm of economics, the expansion of its activity over the entire world, mass production, rationalization, communications and exchange, are not the invention of some liberal or internationalist. They are the essential condition and the basis of any increase in wealth.

This process in history has freely followed its natural course to the moment when the population in Europe grew to such proportions that it was impossible for the peoples to exist under the old economic formulae, without lowering the standard of living. The conquests made during the nineteenth century, which were those of industrial progress, were unquestionably decisive and appear as a phenomenon unique in the history of the world. A century of scientific work and technical progress plus international organization of economy have simply turned to ridicule the old theory that predicted the exhaustion of natural resources and announced famine in the near future as the inevitable fate of the ever-increasing human race.

The providing for humanity of goods in current use and the concession of sufficient leisure profitably used for instruction were before the world wars technically and economically assured, in spite of the continual increase of the population, to such a degree that it would have been impossible to imagine it a hundred years before.

The maintenance and continuation of this progress towards material welfare, economic freedom and cultural achievements depend on a division of labor, rigorously adhered to not only in the heart of each enterprise, but also in the different industries and among the nations, which signifies the distribution of production in the most appropriate places, with freedom of exchange and freedom of migration.

At approximately the same time when this unique process in industrial evolution started, a new ideal was conceived on the basis of the conception of the French Revolution, an ideal which has rooted itself always more deeply in the human soul and mind to such a point that it has become the most powerful religion of our time: Nationalism. In its very nature, nationalism, as understood and cultivated to-day, aspires to *particularization,* to *differentiation,* and divides up humanity more and more rigidly into small units.

These two powerful currents, the integrating evolution of industrialism and the differentiating evolution of nationalism, dominating our epoch, while acting as fire and water, are now tumultuously clashing, and the explosion and conflagration through which we are passing are the consequences of this shock.

The crisis through which we are struggling is a crisis of nationalism and of industrialism. It exploded in July, 1914, and it will terminate either with the collapse of Western industrial civilization, or with the destruction of nationalism as a basis of policy. Such is the alternative that is offered to us.

Nationalism, product of the French Revolution, was in its beginning a high ideal of humanity. Its aim was to liberate the peoples from the domination of absolutism, to proclaim their independence, to transfer the symbol of sovereignty from the king to the people, and to achieve a social order resting on the principles of equality, liberty and justice.

At the end of the eighteenth century, nationalism, as it was conceived by the first founders of modern democracy, was a tremendous step forward. It meant the broadening of the fundaments of the state from one man or a small group to the entire nation. It was the basis of individual freedom, of the rule of law, of free elections, of representative government.

But once established as a basic principle of policy, nationalism had the same fate as all other closed revolutionary ideals, once they ceased to be an ideal and became reality. "The sovereignty of the nation"—a tremendous achievement 150 years ago when industrial progress was still in childhood—began to hurt the realities of the economic life in the second part of the nineteenth century. And since that time, like all social ideals which become dogmas, it has been the greatest obstacle to further progress. It became the popular fate of the uncultured masses, the expression of the lowest instincts of mass inferiority complex, and its defenders are the most intolerant priests of a dogmatic religion we have ever had on this earth.

Nationalism is not a political conception. It does not represent a human ideal any more. It is the principal expression of powerful interests. It possesses all the criteria of a rigorously dogmatic religion, deeply rooted in the soul—deeper than all the disciplines that we readily call religions. The ideals and symbols of nationalism, like the notion of "motherland," "flag," "national anthem," are typical taboos, which today in the highly civilized countries it is more dangerous to touch than the taboos of the savage cannibals of the South Seas. No man, no party dares to touch these relics; no one dares to criticize them. Nevertheless, it must be said that their exalted cult is one of the central roots of the evils of our time.

If a man says loudly and publicly five times daily: "I am the greatest man in the world," everybody will laugh at him, and believe that he is mad. But if he expresses the same psychopathological impulse in the plural and says publicly five times daily: "We are the greatest nation in the world," then he is sure to be regarded as a great patriot and statesman, and will attract the admiration not only of his own nation, but of all mankind.

During the past century three different organizations have tried to fight nationalism without any success: The Catholic Church, the liberal movements, and the international workers' organization.

The eternal ideal of Christianity (which expresses itself in the belief in one sole divinity and in the postulate of peace on this earth) is in absolute contradiction to the ideal of nationalism—this modern religion which rests in reality on the division of humanity into several groups according to origin, race, language and sovereignty, according to the adoration by each nation of a particular god.

The state of affairs that prevails at the present moment in the world would be justly characterized, from the religious point of view, by the term "polytheism." The modern religion of nationalism has driven the Christian faith from the soul of man, and although he goes to mass and attends ceremonies of the Christian Church, the real god to whom he is above all devoted, in whom he has faith, for whom he is ready to fight and give his life, is not the one God of universal Christianity, but the goddess—"Nation."

These gods faithfully resemble the pagan gods of the pre-Christian era. They insist upon the recognition of their race and the hatred of other races. They insist upon war and victory, and they claim vengeance if, instead of victory, it is defeat which comes. England has her god, like France, like the United States, like Germany and Italy; the Russians and the Czechs have theirs, as do the Poles, the Argentines and the Japanese. No matter how small a nation is, it has its own national god.

All these nations hide their pagan instincts under the cloak of Christianity. In all countries nationalism is regarded as a "Christian policy." Everywhere the pagan spirit is cultivated under the moral shield of Christianity falsely interpreted. On all the battlefields where wars rage, Christian priests march before the troops, carrying the symbol of the Son of God—this Son of God who sought peace and love—and it is with the same formula that they bless the two opposing camps that are ready to unleash the fury of their national-pagan passions.

It is undeniable that such a state of affairs must be intolerable to every real Christian, and it is also undeniable that the Church has the greatest interest in seeing its great universal ideal—monotheism—realized, not only in heaven but also on earth amongst peoples.

Unfortunately, the Christian churches, having been frightened by the progress of science, industry and liberalism, thought that their material interests were identical with those forces which were opposing human progress. Frightened by the excesses of the industrial and democratic evolution, as characterized by the doctrines of free masonry and the religious persecutions in Soviet Russia, they lined up more and more with the nationalist forces, until they found themselves, in this great human struggle, allied in many parts of the world with the forces of Fascism, the very essence of which is anti-Christian. Though the policy of the Church is essentially conservative and anti-revolutionary, the leaders of the Christian faith will soon have to realize that they are going to destroy the very principles of Christianity, if they identify themselves for purely material reasons with the various nationalisms which are today fighting in the name of their own particular national gods. Under no condition can the earthly corollary of the ideals of man created in the image of God, charity, tolerance and mercy be racial persecutions, zoological materialism, concentration camps and a cult of aggressive militarism.

The second force which tried to dam the disastrous consequences of dogmatic nationalism was the liberal elements which at the end of the nineteenth century and the beginning of the twentieth century were rather influential among the bourgeoisie of all countries. These elements understood that the state of affairs engendered by nationalism could not be durable, and they strove to break national antagonisms and to bring the peoples together by agreements, treaties and mutual understanding. These tendencies were strongly developed during the years following the First World War and their great achievement was the creation of the League of Nations.

During a certain period, when Briand and Stresemann dominated the international scene, one could almost have believed that they would accomplish their ends. But they failed, justly struck by the iron law, because there are antagonisms, which with the best will in the world and even with the most subtle diplomacy, will not allow themselves to be broken, and because it is impossible to reconcile in treaties and agreements basically irreconcilable forces.

Some people, above all the Anglo-American democracies, harbor even today this ideal which they consider as realizable: voluntary and pacific co-operation of the various sovereign states relying on the "good will" of the peoples. They have stubbornly refused to make any efforts towards a more unified international organization which would bring a weakening of national sovereignty, an international legislation, an international force, commitments, guarantees and sanctions. They proclaimed as the sole basis of work in common the "good will" of the peoples existing or to be created.

This ideal is full of contradictions. If the so-called good will of the peoples existed or were possible as a basis of international relations, it would truly be useless and unnecessary to change or to improve the present organization of the world. Any agreement, treaty or law would be unnecessary if the actions of men or nations were based on what we imagine under the term "good will."

But independently of this simplification of the argument, one has no reason to doubt that each nation is animated by the utmost good will and that it has nothing in view which it does not deem to be just when sitting with the other nations around a conference table. It remains a fact that, in spite of that, the machine does not work.

The reason is clear enough. The idea of "good will" is a figment of the imagination from which nothing can be drawn. Goethe defines in his *Faust,* the nature of the devil as "a part of that power that constantly wishes Evil but which constantly creates Good." Man is at the precisely opposite pole to Mephistopheles. He is a part of that force which constantly wishes Good but which, however, constantly does Evil.

There are no men—if one existed, he would be considered a rare exception—whose actions are inspired solely by evil motives; that is to say, who do not wish well for themselves but who wish ill to their neighbour; who do not wish to defend their own cause which they feel just, but who merely want to destroy the cause of the others. The greatest criminal does not commit a crime to bring harm to others, but in order to secure an advantage to himself, and to carry out an impulse which at a given time appears to him to be right. In spite of this "good will" of men, which unquestionably exists, a social order cannot be imagined without laws of universal force and without compulsory submission of individuals to these laws.

There is no difference whatever between the community of man and the community of nations. No nation taken individually wishes to do harm to the other. All are serving their "justified national interests"; all "defend their country"; all wish "to defend themselves against aggression." It is precisely this deep conviction of the righteousness of one's own interests and demands that has brought the actual chaos and which has rendered its solution impossible. We must try to see clearly into this intricate relationship of motives and acts. We must tread the field of the policy of reality, acknowledge the existing facts and justly gauge the possibilities.

A "rapprochement" between the various sovereign states founded on the principle of nationality and animated by nationalism is impossible. It is pure Utopia. All the attempts at an international rapprochement clashed with the power of nationalism which permits no important concession, either political or economic, without which "international collaboration based on good will" cannot be realized.

One must choose: Either one holds the conception of the national sovereign state which necessarily leads to isolation, to autarchy and ultimately to conflicts and to war; or one wishes to realize an international or at least continental or regional organization which could assure peace and facilitate economic progress. In the latter case, one must get away from the religion of nationalism and its international consequences.

The liberal forces, which during the past decades have become more and more dogmatic, will hardly be in a position to accomplish this fact. They have lost their power in the field of domestic policies because they have converted the ideals of liberalism into a rigid and dogmatic conservative program, thus giving to their adversaries the weapon with which to destroy them. Their views on the organization of international life is just as contradictory to their own principles, as they render to those nations which are opposed to their views the possibility and the means of destroying the democratic peoples who still hold the fundamental ideals of liberalism.

The third and perhaps the most important force which fought nationalism, was the "Internationale" of the Socialist workingmen parties. The proletariat recognized a long time ago that its emancipation could not be attained except by grouping, and it organized its movement on an international basis. Following the motto "Workers of the World Unite," a powerful world-wide party was to be created. It was to realize in all countries the Socialist program in conformity with communal directives.

Already before the First World War, the Socialist Parties were highly developed and making headway. They made considerable progress after the war when, in nearly all European countries, the bourgeois parties with a militaristic, conservative doctrine were breaking up. Millions of men, not only workingmen, but also representatives of the peasantry, of the middle classes and of the intellectuals, belonged to the Socialist Parties from which alone they expected a panacea. After many years of socialistic development and domination, these parties found themselves decadent in nearly all countries. Everywhere they were forced by the discontented masses to give up the capital position which took them so long to conquer.

The policies of the Socialist Parties during the last twenty years brought the greatest deception to the large masses. A great popular movement, which in the beginning gave rise to all hopes, was destroyed when it came into contact with the harshness of reality. The reason why the Socialist Parties were unable to realize even partially their programs, and why they were abandoned so quickly by their followers, is that the "Internationale" was only a fiction.

In all countries where they came to power, the Socialist Parties followed a nationalist policy. All the attempts made with a view to realizing the economic policy of the Socialist program failed as soon as they were subordinated to nationalism, and if something was accomplished, it was only a few achievements of social policy that Bismarck or Lloyd George could just as easily have instituted as the Socialist leaders.

On the other hand, they contemplated an "international rapprochement," conceived on the lines of the liberal wishful thinkers. Never did they dare to fight nationalism in their own country, or they did not wish to. The consequences of this policy, which intended to conquer antagonisms which could not be conquered, have been the lack of success by Socialist governments and those upholding Socialism. The ultra-nationalist and militarist spirit knew in a few years an astounding rebirth. The economic crisis had become catastrophic. The workers, of which the party was supposed to be the real representative, had fallen into a still greater misery. Unemployment rapidly increased, and not only the sympathizers, but many of the original leaders of the Socialist Parties, went over into the camp of the National-Fascist Parties.

The psychology of this process is extremely simple. The power exercised over a long period of years met with no success. The leaders who were nationalists—but not so much so that they could compete with the real apostles of nationalism—threw all the blame on the "foreigners," on the other nations, who were interfering with their policies. It is only natural that the masses rapidly followed the demagogues who fought with all the strength of their hatred "the other nations" and their own democratic government, feeble and without any success to its credit. The Socialist Parties failed because they did not understand that at the present stage of industrial development all the problems raised by the social question can only be solved on the international plan.

So we have witnessed during the past years the triumph of nationalism over Christianity, liberalism and socialism— over all those forces which were opposing it.

Today the world is ruled everywhere by nationalistic forces. The division between nations and their isolation was pushed to an absurd limit, and it is hardly possible to go further in this direction. This ecstasy of nationalism means its end. It is characteristic that even one of the greatest exponents of modern nationalism, Benito Mussolini, when he was still capable of expressing his own views, felt that nationalism, in the actual stage of political and economic development, is no longer a stimulant. He wrote in an article before he attacked Ethiopia, the following phrases: "Nationality as a principle and as the bond in the levelling formation has become the great dynamic force which has contributed to the growth of modern Europe. This force, however, soon ceases to be centripetal; it threatens to change into a centrifugal force and become a factor of disjuncture if it is not held in a state of reasonable equilibrium. It is impossible to exercise complete human justice towards every human instinct and every pride of race. The United States has shown that it is possible to transform into a national formation old sentiments of hatred in one or two generations, if the races, which formerly were animated by an atavistic enmity transmitted from father to son, are united."

Nationalism has actually reached the beginning of its end. It has destroyed and decomposed all that human mind, all that human work had conceived. The absurdity of nationalism is best characterized by the fact that we possess today the technical means of crossing the Atlantic Ocean in seven hours, but it takes seven months to obtain a visa.

Nationalism does not wish to achieve the union of humanity on the basis of 95 per cent of its common characteristics, but to divide it on the basis of 5 per cent of its differentiation. It is the spiritual conception in absolute contradiction to all the conquests realized in the course of the last century. It is the faith which wants to revive the pre-Christian era. It is the enemy of man and is anti-Christian. It is reactionary and makes impossible any progress towards welfare. It is born of terror and fear, of suspicion and mistrust and vanity. It is the most evil epidemic which has attacked humanity. It is the expression of a collective inferiority complex.

It has absolutely nothing to do with the noble feeling, of the love of one's own country, of real patriotism, of which it is a distortion, just as pathological drunkenness is a perversion of the enjoyment of a glass of wine.

It must be understood that there exist only two realities— the *individual* and *humanity*. All other classifications into castes, tribes, classes, religions, races and nations are arbitrary, artificial and superficial.

Nobody can say that these segregations of mankind on whatever basis are fundamental from whatever viewpoint. Frenchmen, Germans and Italians are Swiss patriots. And African Negroes, yellow Chinese, redskin Indians, blue-eyed Irish, dark-haired Greeks and blond Scandinavians are living harmoniously together, with the same feeling of devotion to their country—the United States of America.

We naturally cannot make the skin of the Negro white, and cannot do away with the use of the German language. But we can abolish the principle that it is this arbitrary classification of mankind into races or nationalities which remains the basis of sovereign states. Once we understand this problem and suppress the principle of nationality as the foundation of states, nationalist wars will stop just as automatically as religious wars stopped at the moment when religion was separated from the state and ceased to be its foundation.

# VI

# *Sovereignty*

THE GOLDEN CALF to which the most devoted and mystic adoration of the masses goes in our days is: Sovereignty. No symbol carrying the pretension of a deity, which ever got hold of mankind, caused so much misery, hatred, starvation and mass execution as the notion "Sovereignty of the Nation."

What is Sovereignty?

The appellation comes from the word "sovereign." At the time when peoples were ruled by absolute monarchs, kings, emperors, chiefs, or whatever they were called, it was necessary for them to derive their power from God in order to make people believe and accept that whatever they did, said and ordered was right, infallible and uncontrollable. These attributes were called "sovereign" and the persons vested with them were the "Sovereigns."

For many centuries people suffered under this organization of society, submitted to the uncontrolled, supreme power of monarchs.

The great change came in the eighteenth century, when under the influence of thinkers and philosophers like Locke,

Rousseau, Montesquieu and many others, the masses revolted against their absolute rulers, their Sovereigns.

The revolutionary belief was that "sovereignty resides in the community," and that the notion of sovereignty must pass from the ruler to the nation. This idea was based on the experience of the ancient Greeks and on the conception of Plato, who said that "the state in which the law is above the rulers, and the rulers are the inferiors of the law, has salvation."

This democratic conception of sovereignty had complete victory during the nineteenth century and its aftermath all over the civilized world. The transformation was a most profound one. All dynasties with absolute power—the Bourbons, the Hapsburgs, the Hohenzollerns, the Romanoffs, and many other smaller ruling families—were overthrown; nations accepted the republican form of government; and power was retained only by those royal families who voluntarily gave up their absolute rule and became the symbols of constitutional monarchies, having a function in the state similar to that of presidents in republics.

At the time when the idea of transferring sovereignty from the ruler to the nation was conceived, the industrial revolution had not yet started, modern transportation had not been invented and the term "Nation" was about the widest horizon the fathers of modern constitutions in the eighteenth century could visualize. Their basic idea was to transfer sovereignty from *one* man to *all* the men—to the people—which at that time was identical with the "Nation."

As this idea took form in the modern states, it developed

into something entirely different from what it was meant to be. Through the development of technique and communication, through the economic evolution, the geographical territory to which the sovereignty of the nations extended, became smaller and smaller. Through the political development of many of these nation-states, sovereignty, uncontrolled power, became an institution which did not at all provide for the peoples that freedom, security and happiness that it was meant to. On the contrary, it exerted sovereignty in a way not very different from that of the monarchs. So that at the beginning of the twentieth century, taking the whole world into consideration, the situation was very similar to the anarchic situation of the Middle Ages when feudal landlords exerted sovereign power over their own estates, disregarding entirely the interests of the community of their nations represented by the kings.

The sovereignty of the Nation became more and more a dogma, unchangeable, untouchable, indisputable, on which the whole international relationship had to be based. All attempts to create any kind of international organization to settle the political, the military or the economic relationship between nations failed lamentably, because such a thing as peaceful collaboration among sovereign nations is not conceivable, nor will it ever be obtainable.

We have witnessed the most grotesque manifestations of these attempts. We had various international conferences to lower tariff walls between the nations. The delegates of each sovereign state naturally were concerned only with the best interests of their own country and tried to keep its tariffs as high as possible. Had they acceded to a lowering of their country's tariffs, they would have lost their jobs. But maintaining the sovereignty of their nation by refusing any concession meant that they were able representatives taking good care of the interests of their country.

For many years we followed the deliberations of a disarmament conference called together with the urgent necessity of limiting and reducing national armaments. The assembly was composed of the delegates of the sovereign nations, each one of them having in mind only the safeguarding of his own national interests. Each delegate at the disarmament conference had one thought: to keep for his own country the maximum possible of armaments. Had any of them consented to a reduction in the armaments of their own countries, they would have been considered betrayers, acting disadvantageously to their nations. And when they returned home, after successfully withstanding attempts to reduce national armaments, they were feted as great patriots who had well represented the sovereign rights of their nations to arm without any "foreign interference."

This comedy shortly turned into a tragedy, ending in a catastrophe. But in spite of all this, the sovereignty of the nations cannot be made the subject of discussion, and must be maintained above all and under all circumstances.

So millions will have to die again, hundreds of millions will have to starve again, and billions of dollars will have to be wasted again—because we do not want to recognize that the conception of the sovereignty of nations, which was a great progress in the eighteenth century, did not solve the problem of transferring these sovereign rights from kings to peoples. As long as the sovereignty of the nations has only a geographical limitation and as long as sixty or eighty nations have uncontrolled power and the sovereign right to raise armies, to declare wars, to set tariffs, to stop migration and to exercise that sovereign might over those rights on which depend the entire welfare and happiness of mankind, we cannot say that sovereignty resides in the community.

At the moment when the French Revolution materialized the idea of the Sovereignty of Nation, France was the greatest power in Europe, and her population was half the population of the entire European Continent. She was, according to eighteenth-century conditions, an entirely self-sufficient political and economic entity. But under present-day economic conditions, what sense is there in the "Sovereignty of Latvia," or the "Sovereignty of Luxemburg"?

It will be very hard work to destroy the Golden Calf of Sovereignty for two reasons.

First, the vested interests in the sovereignty of the nations are tremendous. On the small continent of Europe, as it was politically organized in 1919, there were at any time some six hundred members of governments with the title of minister indulging in the exercise of executive power. There were many times that number who were ex-ministers, and as such were holding privileged positions in public life. There were at any time scattered throughout Europe about seven to eight hundred active ambassadors, ministers plenipotentiary, excellencies. Under them there were some ten thousand counsellors, attachés and other functionaries with diplomatic rank. There were at any time about seven to eight thousand legislators, members of parliaments. If we take into consideration only these key men who owe their positions to the existence of their own national "sovereignty," we can easily understand that with all the subordinates, all the personnel required by the administrations of the sovereign states, there were several hundred thousand people, a most powerfully organized caste, who have been directly prospering and existing under the notion of "sovereignty."

But there probably are even greater vested interests in the economic and financial fields. One of the disastrous consequences of sovereignty is the misconception of self-sufficiency or autarchy of each nation. There have been incalculable amounts invested in artificial industries created and maintained through tariff walls in every country in total disregard of any economic law, purely for the purpose of eliminating commerce with other nations and making each unit called a "State" economically independent.

The second reason why the conception of national sovereignty will be hard to do away with—and this is the real difficulty—is a metaphysical one. The sovereignty of the nation is the legal form, the ceremonial expression of the deepest and all-powerful collective inferiority complex we call "Nationalism."

Sovereignty and Nationalism are the two sides of the same false coin. We cannot take one side of it for our services without getting also the other side. Both conceptions in their present form must be destroyed, and an interpretation must be found which will clearly express in terms of twentieth-century realities the meaning given to them when they were instituted in the eighteenth century.

Besides the bewildering confusion and anarchy created

in the political, economic and international fields by the existence of the present "sovereign" states, nationalism and its legal expression, National Sovereignty, cause the greatest amount of friction, confusion and misery also within such individual sovereign states.

With the exception of two or three great countries, hardly any country in the world is composed of one single nationality, and the various conglomerate nationalities are so thoroughly mixed that it is impossible to set up boundary lines so that all the members of a nationality could be settled in one single sovereign state. Consequently, in each sovereign country, besides its own nationality, there are a great many other nationalities, the so-called minorities, creating problems which no sovereign state has ever been able to solve satisfactorily and causing inevitable wars.

If we disregard the latest excesses in religious intolerance of the Nazi and Fascist states, we can state that the religious question has been quite satisfactorily solved during the nineteenth century as a result of the separation of the religions from the sovereignty of the state, as a result of the power put above all religions under which each religion enjoyed equality.

But no state has been able to solve the problem of national minorities, not even the most liberal one. And this problem could not be solved, because there was no sovereign power above the nationalities under which they all could be treated as equals.

There was always one of these nationalities which exerted the sovereign rights of the state over the others. So we have seen that in 1914 the First World War exploded through the revolt of those nationalities and minorities which felt oppressed under the German and Austrian Empires. The victory of the Allies destroyed these empires and "liberated" the Serbs, the Czechs, the Rumanians and the Poles, as well as so many other nationalities. But all of these newly created states merely represented the reverse of the previous order, and there were approximately the same number of men who in 1938 and 1939 revolted against Czech and Polish and Serbian and Rumanian "sovereignty" and thus started the avalanche of a second world war.

The same problem confronts us in India.

The only solution and the only interpretation of sovereignty is to give all nationalities just as we have given all religions total autonomy and full sovereign rights to settle their own cultural, national and local problems. But an organization must be created ranking above them, with full authority to settle all those matters—international relations, military and economic questions—which must be solved in such a way that each nation will have equal rights and equal obligations towards them.

Only through such a *separation of sovereignty,* in establishing national sovereignties for all national matters, and international sovereignties for all international matters, can we create the basis of a world constitution which would really express the democratic thought that "sovereignty resides in the community."

# VII

# *Peace*

THE THIRTY-THIRD SESSION of the Council of the League of Nations met in March, 1925, in the modest surroundings of the dining room of the old Hotel National in Geneva. The order of the day was acceptance by the Council of the Geneva Protocol worked out by the preceding British and French Premiers, MacDonald and Herriot, on the lawns of Chequers. The hopes for a successful League of Nations were still high, and this was the first and only serious attempt to organize collective security within the framework of the League.

At this fateful meeting of the Council, Britain was represented by Sir Austen Chamberlain and France by Aristide Briand. France and all the representatives of the smaller countries at the Council were for acceptance of the Protocol, but everybody knew in advance that Sir Austen Chamberlain, in the name of his newly elected British Conservative Cabinet, would flatly reject it. His arguments were that His Majesty's Government were unable to enter into such general commitments which would tie their hands in the future, that the purpose of the League was to preserve peace and not to prepare for war, and that in the whole project there was too much talk about the possibilities of war . . . "It seems to His Majesty's Government," said Chamberlain, "that anything which fosters the idea that the main business of the League is with war rather than with peace is likely to weaken it in its fundamental task of diminishing the causes of war. . . ."

Briand, trying to put on the best face in the situation, replied to Sir Austen Chamberlain in a witty impromptu speech which created a very gay atmosphere for the interment of the best hope of mankind between the two world wars.

"What is peace?" asked Briand. And he gave his own definition. "According to my philosophy," he said, "peace is nothing but the absence of war."

All of us who were present smiled. Sir Austen Chamberlain was visibly amused at the logic and rhetoric of his eminent French colleague.

This debate between the two greatest Foreign Ministers of Great Britain and France during the post-war period clearly demonstrated how far away the nations were from a clear understanding of the problems of their time.

Until now, peace was indeed nothing but the absence of war, and all the efforts of diplomacy were concentrated merely on adjournments and on compromise solutions of any conflicts arising among the nations. This primitive conception of peace has been prevalent throughout our entire history and particularly in the recent years of exaltation of nationalism and of sovereignty.

During the twenty years preceding this war, we wanted to

preserve peace. We wanted nothing but peace. Believing that peace is merely the absence of a shooting war, and desiring ardently to maintain peace, we were prepared to accept any solution to the problems that arose if only such solutions kept us out of a shooting war.

So we permitted treaties which we signed to be regarded by our enemies as scraps of paper, because insistence on the sanctity of signature would have meant a shooting war. We hypocritically closed our eyes to military aggressions, because we thought that any attempt to prevent such acts of aggression would have meant shooting at us. We called intervention "non-intervention" because we thought if we spoke the truth, it would get us into war. We allowed ourselves to be cheated, to be double-crossed and to be blackmailed because we wanted to keep our peace. And finally the great democratic powers violated even their own commitments and pledges because they thought that peace was more important than honor, decency and confidence in the pledged word.

All the mistakes and blunders committed during the past two fatal decades by the democratic governments were justified by the argument that only by accepting such acts could the democratic peoples preserve their precious peace. We had no policy, no ideals, no purpose, save one—to prevent shooting. We wanted nothing but peace. So the war came.

Whatever we may think of this war, one thing is certain: it is the indisputable and conclusive proof that the policy by which we wanted to preserve peace failed miserably.

As peace was conceived until now—a period without shooting war—it is nothing but the reverse of the Clausewitz definition of war. The more or less short periods of "peace" we have occasionally enjoyed in the past were nothing but the continuation of wars waged by different means. All those brief respites from war which we called "peace" were nothing but diplomatic, economic, political and financial wars between the various groups of men called "nations," with the only distinction that these conflicts, rivalries and hostilities have been fought out with all the means except actual shooting.

If this is what we call peace, if this is what we are aiming at as an ideal, if this is a state of affairs we hope to keep "eternally," or at least for a long time, then peace is a Utopia which we shall never attain, just as it had never been attained in any other period in human history.

But this conception of peace is utterly primitive, outdated and undesirable. There is nothing moral, nothing Christian, nothing civilized, nothing democratic, nothing hopeful in such a status quo.

Whether peace will remain forever a Utopia, or whether it will become a political reality; whether it will remain a hazy dream a thousand years hence, or whether it will be the task of our own generation to realize and organize it, depends entirely upon how we conceive and how we interpret a state of affairs in this world which we would call "Peace."

As a merely negative conception attempting to defend something, as a merely static conception trying to conserve any kind of territorial, political or social order existing or to be created, as a conception of tranquillity and inaction, peace is impossible and will remain forever out of reach. In fact, if that kind of peace could ever be established, it would sound the death knell of progress.

An absence of war for any considerable period between nations organized as sovereign states is impossible. A just international order based on the sovereignty of nations is inconceivable because even if we could at a given moment establish an order which would be felt to be just by all the nations concerned, it would not be the case for long because the essence of life is movement and constant change. To try to keep a peace for more than a short interval between sovereign states possessing arms, merely by diplomacy, means to base the fate of mankind on snake-charming. Against the unalterable realities of history we need more efficient instruments than a flute.

It will be less and less possible to keep nations from shooting at each other as education progresses and more and more nations will claim equality rights with the others.

The claim to equality is almost as old among peoples as the drive for freedom. Equality is another ideal creating a great deal of confusion and misconception.

Since her defeat in 1918, Germany and the other vanquished nations have claimed "equality of rights" as a condition of a pacific evolution. For a decade international policy, and particularly European policy, has been revolving around this principle of "equality of rights."

After long fights, in December, 1932, this principle of equality was granted by the victor nations to the vanquished. Since the granting of this status of equality, the European situation became more chaotic than ever before, and the psychosis of war grew from month to month.

This was the inevitable consequence of the creation of a "basis of collaboration" which was nothing but a fiction and which did not represent any real value.

What does this "equality of rights" mean?

There is hardly an ideal in history which has been abused more often and in a higher degree than the ideal of Equality. And during the past ten years we have seen with our own eyes the most monstrous of these abuses. For Germany the claim for equality was nothing but a technique of imperialistic conquest.

The Germans declared that they had not been treated on an equal footing because they did not have the right to arm as the French, the Poles and the Russians had, and claimed the right for equal armaments. The French declared that in view of their smaller population, freedom for Germany to rearm would put them in a position of inequality. The Germans said that France possessed rich colonies; to which the French replied that Germany disposed of a much more powerful industrial potential. The Germans repeated that France constructed a network of military alliances. To which the French replied that the Germans were training their entire youth for military purposes.

And so on *ad infinitum*.

And even when the Third Reich had already subdued and dominated millions and millions of foreign people, when they had the most powerful armed forces ever created by any nation, their leaders were still clamoring for "equality."

Nobody had the courage to declare publicly that this was a debate in a vacuum without any chance whatsoever of arriving at a satisfactory solution, because this so-called equality was nothing but a subjective feeling interpreted by each government according to its own momentary needs.

Equality is an ideal of the human mind and not something which exists naturally. There is no such thing as equality in Nature, where the stronger always exterminates the weaker. Only when man realized that he was a creature superior to the other animals was equality born as an ideal of man.

But as an ideal of man, equality always needed institutions without which it could not exist. The first great institutions to spread the ideal of equality were the Judaic-Christian religions with their postulate that man has been created in the image of God and that all men are equal before God. This principle enunciated many thousand years ago shows the only form in which equality can find expression. This is *equality before a certain specific authority, under a concrete symbol*.

There have been many attempts in the course of the centuries to establish equality among men in the political or social field. With one single exception, they have always failed. Only the French Revolution and the revolutions in connection with it have been able successfully to enact legislation for equality, in guaranteeing equality to the citizens *before the law*. This interpretation of equality—equality before the law—was always self-evident in English common law.

The reason for this success was that the Fathers of the Revolution followed the same practice as the Fathers of Christianity. They did not want to institute "general equality" among men, which does not exist and never will exist, but they wanted to establish equality in a limited and specified field, in the field of jurisdiction, and they made all men equal before the courts, before law, just as Christianity made men equal before the symbol of God.

In many fields inequality remained unchanged in the relationship among men. There was still a difference between strong and weak men, poor and rich men, clever and stupid men, but before the laws of the state they were made equal.

In the general claim for equality among nations, we have now arrived at the stage where we must clearly define what we understand under equality of nations. The present interpretation of "equality," the right to do what the others do, the right to arm to the same extent as the others do, the right to possess just a little more arms than the others have (because otherwise, the others might possess a little bit more and thus there will be no "equality"), is such nonsensical logic that it is not necessary to waste any time in discussing it.

There will always be differentiation between nations, just as there will always be differentiation between individuals. And it is essential for cultural progress that such differentiation should persist.

Equality of nations is just as much of an ideal of civilization as equality among men. In itself it is against nature and can only be attained through the proper institutions.

*Equality without law has no sense and no moral justification whatsoever.* This is valid for both the social and the international life. It is only law that makes equality possible, and only before clearly specified laws can we make nations, just like men, equal.

Without law, the drive for equality in international life is the greatest danger and direct cause of wars.

Without international law, the drive for equality among nations leads towards armaments, towards alliances, towards coalitions. Between two neighboring nations, one will always be weaker than the other. First they compete in increasing armaments. When this race reaches its optimum they begin to seek alliances with other nations. The process which has been repeated over and over again in history was called the search for a "balance of power." It always led and must continue to lead to wars.

Equality without law means war.

The only way to maintain peace for a certain period without law is the domination of one nation by another, the supremacy of one group of powers over the others.

The only possibility of maintaining peace and of giving the nations equality is the establishment of law under which each nation has to be equal.

Therefore, the cardinal point in the definition of peace is: *Law*.

Only if we are decided to enact international laws having the same characteristics as national laws, binding all nations, or at least a certain number of nations, can we lay the foundation for a peaceful development in international relations. Any conception of peace without mandatory international law is a hopeless dream. The criterion of any realistic interpretation of peace is its foundation on law.

Peace is not an end in itself. It cannot be achieved by wanting it for itself. It is the reward for a right and just policy. Nobody who has no idea other than to become rich or famous ever has any chance of achieving his aims. Fortune, fame, comfort, security are not gained by wanting them for their own sake; they are rewards which come to those who are active and useful, and who produce something which is useful to others. They are only the accompanying results of talent, diligence, perseverance and creativeness. Only those who have creative ideas and concentrate their efforts on productive work have any chance of becoming successful in life.

If we want peace and nothing but peace, we shall never have it. Peace is the result of positive, creative and constructive policy. And any positive, constructive and creative policy today begins with the realization that we have to give up those views on the fundamental principles of international life which have been proven to be obsolete, and to give them interpretations in accordance with the realities of our time.

The usual distinction between national law and international law, the former having coercive force, the latter without such coercive force, is a purely theoretical definition. It has no practical value whatsoever.

"International law," as we know it, is merely a system of norms, customs, rules, treaty obligations, without compulsive power. It is no law at all. It is a game. To call it "law" only makes the problems of international relationship even more confused.

Most of our statesmen and authorities on law believe that the problem of peace can be solved on the basis of such "international law." It has been tried several hundred times in history. The time has come when we must realize that we have been running after a Fata Morgana.

What we used to call "international law" is no law at all, and it is important to avoid the use of this term in describing present and past international conditions. We must limit the term "law" to measures with coercive power. And we shall only be able to talk about "international law" when we establish a system of norms in the relationship between nations with the same executional force as in national law. The organization of peace on the basis of that hypothetical international law which we have known until now and which is merely a custom or a treaty obligation has never succeeded and can never succeed.

There can be no peaceful relationship among the nations without a machinery to determine cases of "delict," and there can be no peace without the possibility of reprisals against such delicts.

Only the existence of law makes a certain action a delict. And only the existence of law makes a certain measure a "sanction."

The recognition of a delict and the application of sanctions which form the bases of any legal order—both presuppose the existence of law.

The history of social progress shows that the use of force in the relationship between individuals within an organized state can be abolished only by instituting the employment of force by law in all cases where an individual member of the state commits an illegal act.

International order based on law means exactly what

national order means in the social life. It means that the use of force is prohibited for the individual, but, under specified conditions and in specified forms, it is permitted for the community.

To institute legal employment of force by a central authority among nations is regarded by many as Utopian. However, it is the only solution to the problem. On the contrary, any scheme which suggests solving the problem of peace without the legal use of force in international affairs is Utopian, as history definitely teaches. It has always been tried. It has never worked. And it will never work.

Peace is law.

Law is the justified use of force—a coercive order.

Consequently, peace without the employment of force is inconceivable.

# VIII

## *War*

THE CENTRAL PROBLEM of all our controversies is, of course, the problem of war. This problem is as old as human history itself. In fact, the history of mankind is nothing but the history of wars.

With the exception of convinced militarists and the adherents of a modern form of paganism represented by the Fascist-Nazi movements, the great majority of people of all races have a deep feeling that war is something evil, something wrong, a sort of catastrophe, and they all desire peace.

This feeling also is probably as old as human history. But in spite of the fact that the overwhelming majority of mankind has loathed war and wanted peace for thousands of years, history shows that there have been fewer warless years on this planet during the past centuries than years in which some sections of the human race were waging wars.

It seems that there is some truth in the famous Clausewitz definition that war is the continuation of policy by other means. If we disregard the older ages and look at the development of the last century, since the end of the Napoleonic wars, it appears clearer and clearer that the spread-

ing of education, science, communications, makes more and
more people believe that war is something that must be
abolished. No government in any of the civilized countries
was able to obtain the support of the majority of its people
with a program of war. All governments promised peace.
They all had to promise to fight against war and they all
were able to bring their nations into war only by making
them believe that they were attacked and were merely defending themselves. In spite of this growing feeling for international peace, mankind was driven into more devastating wars than ever before.

Why can't we stop wars if people really want to abolish
them?

In order to be able to answer this question, we must first
put another and simpler question: What is war?

The popularly accepted answer to this question is that
war is a struggle between two groups of people with
weapons.

If this is how we understand war; if we mean by war
simply the killing of poeple, the destruction of each other's
properties, fighting and struggling for some purpose, then
we shall never be able to abolish wars. If we interpret war
in this primitive fashion, then our desire to abolish it is
childish Utopia. According to this definition, war is the
application of force by nations, and you cannot abolish the
use of force which emanates from deep instincts and passions and which lies in human nature itself.

We have never been able to abolish individual crime, the
use of brutal force between individuals, though we have

been trying to do so since the beginning of organized society, since the beginning of religion.

But what we were able to accomplish as regards individual crimes in organized society was to make it clear through certain legislation what actions were regarded as crimes and in setting up the necessary organization, legislation, jurisdiction and police execution to reduce such criminal actions to a minimum, and through retribution for crimes to create a feeling of individual security among citizens.

War as a struggle between peoples, as the explosion of human passions, as the dynamic factor in human history, cannot and never will be abolished.

But if we take into consideration the evolution of individual murder, theft, fighting within an organized state, we cannot accept such a simplified definition of wars as is generally accepted today all over the world.

We make a very clear differentiation between the man who kills someone in order to get a thousand dollars out of his victim's pocket and the man who executes someone on the basis of a legal document which we call a judgment. Though the two acts are from a biological point of view absolutely identical, we generally do not call them both murder.

The same differentiation must be admitted and clearly stated with regard to the process of killing by groups of people we generally call wars.

We shall be unable to abolish war through any imaginable organization, just as we have been unable to abolish murder despite all the might of an organized police force.

We might be in a position to reduce international wars to a minimum through an appropriate organization of the peoples, just as we have been able to reduce murder cases in a civilized state to an absolute minimum.

The basis of such an organization must be a clear and unmistakable definition of what we understand by the kind of war we want to abolish. We must make a distinction between *legal* and *illegal* wars. Our only possibility of abolishing illegal wars seems to be the acceptance and the legalization of certain kinds of warlike actions which we shall have to resort to if we want to get rid of such devastating world wars as our generation has witnessed twice.

Above all, we must give up all those primitive ideas we have been following during the past decades, in order to "humanize" wars. This is a total waste of time and an utterly naive conception of our present age. As long as wars were decided upon and waged by monarchs, mostly with professional armies, it was possible to establish certain "rules" for such wars, as though they were fencing-school duels. But since the modern wars of conscription involve the entire populations of the nations, all such rules are impracticable and without any value. It is obvious that in any such war every nation will apply all weapons which it believes might bring victory in the shortest possible time. All the rules, therefore, which have been established by various conventions as to the use of certain weapons, as to the bombardment of the civilian population, as to submarine warfare, are nothing but wishful thinking in times of peace, to which no army pays any attention once engaged in a modern war.

We might be able to prevent a certain type of international war through a definite policy, legislation and application of force, but we shall certainly never be able to "humanize" war once it has broken out.

The same naive idea of preventing wars is the idea of disarmament which has been so passionately advocated by pacifists from 1919 to 1935, until the complete breakdown of the Disarmament Conference. To believe that we shall be able to maintain peace by reducing the caliber of the guns, the tonnage of warships, or the number of trained soldiers is naive indeed. As if we did not have wars before the 40,000-ton dreadnoughts, before the 16-inch guns and before the armies of millions.

If we are going to maintain an international society composed of sovereign states without any legal organization, then we are going to have periodical wars just as we had in the past, no matter what kind of weapons we permit them to use, and we can be certain that each nation will use all the weapons modern science and industry can make available to them.

We can never get rid of wars through disarmament. Disarmament can only be the consequence of an international organization to prevent illegal wars. In fact, if we regard armaments as causes of wars, the lesson history teaches is that only inequality of armaments was able to maintain peace for a certain time. Equality of armaments always meant and probably always will mean war.

One of the most erroneous conclusions we can draw from history is to regard peace and war as two different things, as two opposite poles, as two conditions which exclude each other. In fact, they seem to be fluctuations of one and the same aspect of human society, just as cold and hot are both temperature, only in a different degree. In order to create the temperature best suited to human organism sometimes we must add heat; sometimes we must reduce heat. In the well-organized international order we are aiming at, we shall have to undertake from time to time warlike actions in order to maintain and strengthen social balance and international peace.

The most powerful argument of the dogmatic pacifists, of the adherents to the disarmament theory and of the non-interventionists, was that "you cannot prevent war by waging war."

This is a most dangerous sophism. In fact, the only way to prevent illegal and anarchic wars is to wage a certain kind of *legal* war, just as the only way to fight and reduce crime is to commit the same "crimes" on a legal basis against the criminals.

This legalization of a certain type of wars has nothing to do with the notion of *Bellum Justum,* used for centuries in debates on international law.

Statesmen and jurists used to call *Bellum Justum* a war of reprisal, a "justified" war against the state responsible for an illegal act.

This term is a purely subjective notion and has no practical sense. In fact, all wars in history were so prepared that the soldiers and nations who fought them were convinced that they were fighting a *Bellum Justum.* Every war of every nation was fought for a "righteous cause," for "justified national interests" and "in self-defense." Indeed, this theory justifies *all wars,* and therefore is merely a sophistic argument, a wholly unsatisfactory explanation of the past wars.

Legal wars which we have to institute if we want to abolish illegal wars presuppose the existence of an international legal order.

They mean forceful military actions undertaken in the name of the community, with the authority of the community, for the maintenance and safeguard of the established legal order.

# IX

## *Non-Intervention*

THE DOCTRINE that perhaps wrought the most havoc in international relations is the principle of non-intervention. This principle, which is so deeply rooted in the minds of our statesmen and diplomats that it can be called a dogma, is in such complete contradiction to every manifestation of the modern life of nations that its consequences during the past twenty years have been disastrous. This doctrine was one of the main reasons why a band of unscrupulous gangsters was able to achieve supreme power in Europe.

The principle of "non-intervention in the internal affairs of other countries" was established centuries ago by hereditary monarchies. It was a question of courtesy among gentlemen, expressing the same feeling as many related families have towards each other's domestic affairs. The nations were ruled by old, historical dynasties. War and peace were decided upon by the monarchs, and it was the understanding among the great ruling houses that they were not to interfere with each other's internal affairs. At that time it was a defensible principle.

During the period of transition from absolute monarchies

to democratic nations, this idea was taken over, as it was to the interest of the newly established democracies that the remaining kings should not interfere in their internal constitutional life. But as time went on and the development of industry, commerce and communications made one single economic unit of the whole world, this principle of non-intervention in the internal affairs of other countries became a farce.

It has the same effect on our international life as Prohibition had on the public life of the United States. Being entirely in contradiction to reality, it not only does not safeguard a nation from foreign intervention, but makes it subject to all kinds of illegal intervention.

It is not necessary to enumerate all the cases in which, under the hypocrisy of non-intervention, the totalitarian powers interfered in the internal affairs of other countries, established their own organizations, undermined the existing social order, bribed and corrupted men and institutions, instigated and fostered assassinations, revolutions and civil wars.

Hardly any nation on this earth was exempt from these internal convulsions. But the democratic countries closed their eyes to these facts, saying that this was none of their business, that they could not do anything because any action would be against the principle of non-intervention. And this principle was sacrosanct.

But apart from the great number of catastrophes which were the direct result of "non-intervention," what are the possibilities of a policy based on that principle, and what is the real relationship of the internal affairs of the nations towards each other?

Let us regard the world as it was established and organized after the First World War. Those who created that order believed that they laid the foundation for a closer international relationship, for better distribution of wealth, for increased international commerce, for disarmament, prosperity and permanent progress. And what happened?

The newly created states started with a policy of "self-sufficiency." Czechoslovakia, which inherited the great industrial enterprises of the former Austro-Hungarian monarchy, was predominantly an industrial country. Hungary as it remained was a purely agricultural country. For years the Czechoslovakian Government pursued a one-sided agricultural policy, creating by mainly artificial means and subventions a domestic agriculture, in order to produce at home the necessary foodstuffs, with the consequence that Hungary and the other Balkan countries lost a natural market for their agricultural surpluses and were unable to buy industrial products from Czechoslovakia and from other industrial countries. As an "only remedy" they started to create, equally by purely artificial means and government subventions, a new industry in order to produce at home whatever products their farmers needed. The result was rising prices and lowered living standards in all the countries concerned.

When as a result of the world economic crisis Britain gave up the gold standard and devaluated sterling, the United States shortly after was forced to devaluate the dollar proportionately.

When the Disarmament Conference started and the democratic nations were prepared and willing to reduce their armaments, Italian militarism and intensified German armaments thwarted every attempt at an agreement and forced the democratic nations also to rearm.

The examples could be multiplied almost without limit. In each case we see that the internal policy of a certain government or governments—economical or financial, in the labor or military field—forced other governments to adapt their own policies to the new conditions created by the others.

The richest country in the world—the United States of America—abounding in plenty in the production of consumers goods, and where the supply of raw materials seemed to be inexhaustible, was forced to stop motor-car production for private consumption, to ration sugar, to conscript its entire man power, to limit individual income, to tax all excess profits, thus changing most radically the American way of life.

Why?

These revolutionary changes in the mighty United States of America, so self-assured in its power, in its political and economic superiority, and in its aloofness from the "foreign quarrels," are the *direct consequences* of the fact that a few years before the German Government stopped motor-car production for private use, conscripted its youth, rationed sugar, taxed excess profit and limited individual income. Yet, there are people in the United States who, after having witnessed how the internal policy of a country 4,000 miles away has directly and profoundly affected the internal policy of the United States and the daily life of its citizens, are still talking seriously about non-intervention as a "policy"!

If one nation pursues an autarchic policy, it disrupts the entire international trade and affects the living standard of every individual of the other nations. If one nation enters into an armament race, every other nation is forced to spend a bigger portion of its national income for armaments. If one nation regards a treaty as a scrap of paper, treaties in general lose their value. If one great nation devaluates its currency for internal financial reason, other nations are forced to follow suit. If one government is in a position to force its workers to work sixty hours a week, it reacts on labor conditions in other countries. If one nation begins to educate its youth on a purely militaristic basis, all the other nations have to prepare for military organization. If one government exploits without scruple the advantages of dictatorship, all the other nations are forced to renounce more and more of their democratic achievements.

The internal lives of the individual nations are so interwoven, their effect upon each other so apparent, that this interchange of causes and effects is one of the few crystallizations of international life which has the characteristics of a social law.

And this law seems to be a very peculiar one. It resembles in some respects the theory of marginal utility in economics, whereby the price of a commodity is determined by the cost of production to the producer, working under the least favorable conditions among those able to compete.

It seems that in the modern inter-related lives of the nations the standard of living, of culture, labor conditions, in-

dividual freedom, taxation, export trade, defense policy—
all depend to a great extent on the policies followed in the
same fields by other nations. And the nation living under
the lowest moral and least favorable economic conditions is
the determining factor.

It appears that in a given territory—certainly on the continent of Europe, but probably on the entire globe—there
exists some law or at least some tendency according to
which, among a certain number of interdependent nations,
all the states are forced to adapt their form of government
to the least civilized form of government existent in any
state among them.

# X

# *Neutrality*

AT THE PAN-AMERICAN CONFERENCE at Rio de Janeiro, Mr.
Sumner Welles, the representative of the United States of
America, in an address before twenty-one South American
Republics, on January 15, 1942, made the following declara-
tion:

"The record of the past two years is ever before us. You
and I know that had there existed during the past decade
international order based upon law, and with the capacity to
enforce such law, the earth today would not be subjected
to the cruel scourge which is now ravaging the entire globe.
Had the law-abiding and peaceful nations of Europe been
willing to stand together when the menace of Hitlerism
first began to become manifest, Hitler would never have
dared to embark upon his evil course. It was solely because
of the fact that these nations, instead of standing together,
permitted themselves to hold aloof one from the other, and
placed their hope of salvation in their own neutrality, that
Hitler was enabled to overrun them one by one as time and
circumstances made it expedient."

The representative of the United States Government declared further:

"The shibboleth of classic neutrality in its narrow sense can, in this tragic modern world, no longer be any real neutrality as between the powers of evil and the forces that are struggling to preserve the rights and independence of free peoples. It is far better for any people to strive gloriously to safeguard its independence; it is far better for any people to die, if need be, in the battle to save its liberties than, by clinging to the tattered fiction of an illusory neutrality, succeed only by so doing in committing suicide."

These words uttered by the representative of the United States of America are the most tragic self-condemnation of one's own former policy ever pronounced by a government.

These were precisely the words with which Great Britain and France tried to persuade the United States of America about the vanity, inefficiency and emptiness of its neutrality policy during the past years. These were the very words the Spanish, Austrian and Ethiopian Governments vainly repeated over and over to the British and French Governments. These were the very words which fell on deaf ears and had no effect at all when the Czechs addressed them to the Poles, the Poles to the Scandinavians, the Greeks to the Yugoslavs, and the Yugoslavs to the Turks.

Today, when the "policy of neutrality" is a dismal failure all over the globe, when no neutral nation—with the exception of a few minor countries—escaped aggression, war and conquest through its neutrality, it is no more great statesmanship to admit that neutrality is suicide.

The fact remains that not one nation gave up its neutrality in this world conflict, until it was forced to do so; that no nation admitted any criticism of its policy of neutrality, and that no democratic power dared to touch the dogma of neutrality, even *during* the war when in many cases it was obvious that the proclamation or recognition of neutrality was the surest road to military defeat. So we have witnessed not only the Manchurian-Ethiopian-Spanish farce in times of "peace," but also the tragi-comedy of landing British troops in Greek ports under the eyes of German diplomats and of the operating of the British Middle East headquarters in Cairo under the constant watch of Axis diplomatic representatives on the spot.

The active help given to the dictatorial powers in this war by the principle of neutrality is immeasurable.

The series of non-aggression pacts and neutrality guarantees signed and proclaimed by Hitler during the past years, thus permitting the conquest of all the countries which he never could have conquered if they had been united, but which he swallowed up one by one, was the greatest triumph of seduction since Casanova and Don Juan. The victims were made all the more ridiculous, as each one of them from the tiny Luxemburg to the mighty United States believed profoundly that they would be treated differently and that the saccharine words Hitler addressed to them were in their special cases really sincere.

The dogmatic belief in neutrality is so strong that even today, after the conquest of so many countries due entirely to their neutrality, many representatives of those countries, Poles and Dutch, Rumanians and Norwegians, defend their old futile policy, maintaining that neutrality in itself was right and they could not have followed any policy other than the one they did follow.

As there is little chance that people will learn from experiences, however tragic and however close such experiences may be to them, it is almost certain that they will return again to this policy unless we realize the utter historic, moral and political impossibility of the principle of neutrality.

The idea of neutrality stems from those ages when wars were recognized as legal acts of policy, when wars were fought among dynasties, among countries for frontier changes and for colonial expansion. In those periods when wars were generally limited to two or a few participants, when they never went beyond certain geographical boundaries, when they were fought under certain accepted regulations, and ended usually in negotiation and reconciliation, it was possible to establish a principle whereby certain wars did not touch nations outside the conflict or its dangers.

But since the technical developments and the industrial evolution have reduced the earth to a small unit; since the wars are no longer fought for reasons of dynastic jealousies or for local controversies; since we are in a great struggle for power to put the earth, or at least major parts of it under unified control; since the democratic nations are trying to organize this struggle for world power without bloodshed, and are trying to outlaw wars by calling them a crime, neutrality is not only political nonsense, but the greatest moral turpitude.

It is a total contradiction to qualify certain acts of the totalitarian regimes as criminal and to declare the intention to remain neutral before the drama that is unfolding.

Every declaration of neutrality sanctions the actions of

the Fascist, Nazi and Japanese militarists, because it expresses implicitly the assumption that the violations of international morality committed by the totalitarian forces permit an attitude of neutrality.

What is really revolting in the tragic events of the past ten years is not the repeated breach of faith, treachery, aggression, brutal conquest and the enslavement of hundreds of millions of people by the totalitarian governments, but the attitude of those people in the civilized, Christian countries who possess the moral capacity to recognize that we are faced with the most outrageous crimes ever committed on this earth under any form, and who in spite of the realization of the truth believe themselves to be entitled to say: This does not concern us; we want to stay out.

Whatever the excuse for such an attitude may be, whether it is fear, cowardice, indifference or blindness, from an ethical point of view it is beyond doubt that those who have the moral strength to recognize the crime, and yet tolerate it, are more guilty than those who commit the crime.

# XI

## *Independence*

THE LONGING for freedom as a natural drive in the individual
finds its parallel in the drive for independence in the lives of
nations. Indeed, the impulse towards national independence
is just as powerful a natural drive in history as the impulse
for individual freedom. Just as the French Revolution was
the greatest symbolic event in the liberation of the individual and in proclaiming the Rights of Man, the greatest symbolic event in the obtainment of national independence
from foreign rule was the American Revolution and the
Declaration of Independence. These two great revolutions
had the same root and were based on the same principles.
The Declaration of the Rights of Man and of the Citizen,
and the Declaration of Independence were both based on
the "Laws of Nature," on certain inalienable rights, on
equality, liberty, fraternity, and on life, liberty and the pursuit of happiness.

The drive for national independence has gained tremendous strides during the nineteenth century and reached
its climax in the peace treaties of 1919, when—at least in
Europe and America—each nation, even the smallest one,

became independent. It was the basic principle of the order created in 1919 that each nation, regardless of its size, had the right to organize its independent national life, as the United States of America, Great Britain and the French Republic organized their national lives, according to the principles of the eighteenth century. The Czechs, Lithuanians, the Poles and Rumanians became independent, and in 1920 more nations than in any other period in history achieved complete independence.

What became of this widely spread independence?

Twenty years later more nations than ever before were subjugated either by direct military conquest or by other means of political domination. And this modern kind of subjugation has been more relentless than any other form of dependence before the great revolutions for freedom and independence.

Why was it impossible for so many nations to keep their independence longer than a mere few years?

The answer is a very simple one. The total independence of all the nations created in the international life as anarchic a situation as would be inevitable in any state in which there was total freedom of the individual, without any restrictions, without any laws, without compulsion.

Wilson, Col. House, Masaryk, Lord Cecil, Leon Bourgeois, and the other encyclopedists of the 1919 treaties, thought that each nation would be happy to be independent and that through collaboration of these independent states, based on mutual good-will, we could maintain peace, organize international life and develop human progress. They entirely disregarded a great number of forceful impulses in human nature just as "natural" as the drive for freedom and independence, which, if not regulated, controlled and checked, bring more misery into the lives of "independent" nations than the worst kind of slavery.

They completely disregarded the fact that political independence of each national state is incompatible with present economic conditions. And so we witnessed in the short period between 1920 and 1940 that the world as it was made safe for democracy was incapable of preventing a reaction to the democratic ideas, to the ideas of self-determination, of independence and of equality, more violent and more volcanic than any other change in history in such a short time.

The independence of the nations was a taboo, and no independent government was prepared to make international commitments, fearing that any such commitment might jeopardize the independence of their country. There was no binding international law and there was no organization to compel the nations to obey such law. Consequently, the governments of the independent nations distrusted each other and intrigued against each other, just as the absolute monarchs did when they ruled over subjugated peoples.

Each independent nation was dominated by the deep, natural impulse which we call fear and which is the root of so many evil human actions. Through fear, mutual mistrust and jealousies which no appeal to reason has ever been able to eradicate, natural conflicts arose among nations just as they arose when they were not independent. In each case where such a conflict arose, the independent governments met to study the factors involved and to determine who was responsible. There being no law and no generally accepted definition for such cases, they exchanged their own subjective views, each one, of course, trying to defend the interests of his own nation. Obviously, they never arrived at any practical conclusion; the solution of each one of those conflicts was put off, with the result that the number and the gravity of these conflicts grew in geometrical sequence.

The same juridical persons, the "representatives" of the independent nations, were in international life the legislators, the judges and the executors. The idea was that a gathering of the representatives of such independent governments should fulfill all the three functions of a democratic international life. This primitive conception of international life based on national independence led from conflict to conflict, until in the case of Italian aggression in Ethiopia, world opinion was aroused to a point which made some sort of action unavoidable.

For the first time it was attempted to apply sanctions against a great power violating the independence of another nation. The procedure was based on such an improvised collaboration of nations. The result was a total failure. Nobody explained more clearly the reasons for this failure than the former French President, Millerand, in a speech in the French Senate on June 26, 1936. The Nationalist French statesman, urging the recognition of the Mussolini conquest, said: ". . . In reality, the cause of the failure of the sanctions is entirely different. In order to understand it, it is sufficient to remember that there is not one nation in the world which would consent to wage war, a modern war, except in the case when its vital interests were involved, when its national independence is threatened, and its frontiers menaced."

This reasoning is the natural expression of a conception of independence we have established in the past and to which most of our statesmen still adhere.

It was best explained by Senator Borah while he was Chairman of the Foreign Relations Committee of the American Senate.

The Senator from Idaho said: "There are some things in this world more to be desired than peace, and one of them is the unembarrassed and unhampered and untrammeled political independence of this republic—the right and power to determine in every crisis, when that crisis comes, untrammeled by any previous commitments, the course which it is best for the people of this nation to pursue. If peace cannot be had without our surrendering that freedom of action, then I am not for peace."

It is to be hoped that the catastrophe in which we find ourselves today as a result of such an interpretation of independence will cause some of our leaders to think about this problem in present-day terms, in relation to the present-day trends and realities of the world, and to see whether the expression of independence, as it is codified today in democratic constitutions, does help us to a better life, liberty and the pursuit of happiness for the purpose of which it was proclaimed.

Today political independence has no sense without economic independence. And economic independence obviously cannot be obtained by any single nation. We used to believe that there are at least two or three big nations in the world which can call themselves economically independent. But the present war has shown that not even the United States of America, not even Soviet Russia, is economically independent.

In the presence of these revealing facts, proving that no nation, not even the mightiest, can achieve economic independence, we must realize that at the present stage of history, political independence is no more an ideal which can help us in attaining our goal. As a practical institution, it is catastrophic.

# XII

## *Inter-dependence*

EVERY MAN is born into the greatest of all dependencies—into the dependency of the family.

At the beginning of his life every child is totally helpless and he depends entirely upon the care of his mother. He would die on the first day of his existence were it not for the care given to him by his parents.

The role of the father in the family is the role of an absolute monarch.

Every child is the slave of his family. He gets from it his food, his shelter, his clothes and he has to do what his parents tell him without the right of questioning why.

But as soon as the child grows up, he is seized by a tremendous desire to become independent of family ties. Every man remembers that period of his life as a restive and most rebellious one, ending in the cutting of the family bonds.

Hardly does a man become "independent" of the family, when the whole outlook changes. Independence does not give the satisfaction one anticipates. It gives instead a feeling of aloneness, doubt, uncertainty, fear. And in a very short time new drives begin to torment the soul of a young man, as a reaction to his independence: a drive for new commitments, a drive for creating a new family, a drive to be a member of society, of a trade union, of a party.

The new drive that overwhelms every individual as soon as he reaches maturity is the drive to become inter-dependent with his fellow citizens.

This evolution—*dependence, independence, inter-dependence*—is the natural process of life through which every individual has to pass.

And this very same process represents also the stages through which nations pass in their historic development. We are now at the stage when complete independence brought the greatest disillusions to most nations, when it collapsed as an ideal, and when the nations have some kind of feeling of the insufficiency and futility of this ideal.

The transition is a terrible crisis in the life of a nation, just as it is a tragic moment in the life of an individual. But it is of the utmost importance that we recognize the real nature of this crisis, in order to avoid its exploitation by unscrupulous movements seeking to create new forms of enslavement of nations on the ground that national independence, as an ideal for man as it was interpreted during the past decades, had collapsed.

The total independence of nations as it was established after the First World War created the same feelings in the collectivity as total freedom creates in the life of a man—the feeling of doubt, the feeling of insecurity and the feeling of fear, which are the origin of armaments, militarism and conquests.

Only through a new integration and inter-dependent organization of the nations can these drives be overcome, and can national freedom and national independence find their true expression.

In the early stages of our society, the people understood that freedom can only be a practical institution among individuals if it is limited and regulated by law. But this evidence has not been recognized in the economic field. Here, during the nineteenth century and the first part of the twentieth century, we understood freedom as "absolute freedom," and regarded for a long time thoughts and movements tending to limit and organize economic freedom as "anti-democratic." The result of it was a growing economic anarchy, and, in spite of ever-increasing production, a growing feeling of individual economic insecurity, poverty and unemployment.

As a reaction to such absolute economic freedom which we wanted to maintain, there arose in the masses a drive for compulsion which is the origin of all the totalitarian movements. It is no explanation to call the Fascist and Nazi movements "criminal" or "insane." They are the natural reaction to a false interpretation of the conception of independence. However difficult it may be for freedom-loving people to understand, longing for compulsion is just as natural a drive in human nature as longing for freedom and can only be checked by a correct interpretation of this ideal.

The total independence of nations, as we understood it until now, does not guarantee the freedom of nations for the simple reason that total independence of nations means not only that a nation can do whatever it wants, but that other nations are also completely free to do whatever they like.

Such a situation, far from securing independence for the nations, is international anarchy in which each nation must always be prepared to be economically ruined or militarily invaded by any other nation at any time.

It is, therefore, obvious that a much higher degree of independence of the nations would be attained if certain phases of such total independence were limited, regulated and properly controlled for all of them, and if these limitations and regulations were enforced on all of them by institutions *above* all of them.

The optimum of national independence is relative and rests on two factors:

First, to what degree a nation is independent itself.

Second, to what degree a nation is exposed to the interfering actions of other independent nations.

We have already seen that if a nation starts to rearm, all other nations have to do likewise. If a nation proceeds to a currency devaluation, all nations in their economic relationship must do the same. If a nation forces its laborers to work twelve hours a day at starvation wages, no social progress is possible in other countries. If a nation establishes a dictatorship, the freedom of all the other countries is directly menaced.

In the face of all these facts in recent years which prove the indisputable correctness of this thesis, it should no longer be possible for civilized people to stand idly by when a government is terrorizing its people, is persecuting millions of men, is violating the most elementary laws of Christian morals, is spreading hatred, is rearming, and preparing for foreign military conquests, until the disease becomes incurable and a general breakdown occurs.

It should become more and more plain that the internal system of a country determines its "foreign policy," and that the internal regime of each country has a direct effect on all the other countries.

Our foreign policies are still based on the dogma that the internal affairs of a country do not concern the other countries and that the international conduct of a government is what counts in the relationship among nations, and not its internal policies.

This thought is the remnant of those good old days of diplomacy among gentlemen, when differences were merely formal and external. Indeed, constitutional monarchies and constitutional republics can live peacefully side by side and can follow the policy of non-intervention in each other's internal affairs.

But nations with a democratic form of government and governments whose declared purpose is to destroy democratic principles everywhere; nations who respect treaties and signatures, and nations who despise such formalities; nations who abhor the use of force, and nations who worship force—such nations cannot live peacefully together, if all of them are independent and if their independence is not controlled or limited in any way. In such an international situation war is inevitable.

The differences that divide humanity today and that have caused the present war are much deeper and more funda-

mental than those conflicts which were easily solved in the
past with superficial diplomatic formulae.

The needless sufferings which mankind has to go through
today will perhaps make it possible to organize international life on the basis of inter-dependence, which is the
only form in which we can find a way out of the present
convulsion. The opportunity is *now,* during this world-wide
struggle, which involves every nation and when every
nation realizes that its independence as it was interpreted
until now did not give them national freedom and security.

We shall solve no problem by calling the Germans, Japanese and Italians and their satellites, gangsters or Huns or
apes. The problem is how and why those gangsters, Huns
and apes were able to grow as all-powerful as they did before
our very eyes. And how and why they were able to cause
the conflagration of the entire planet.

In order to lay the foundation of a world order in which
such destruction and such catastrophes would be impossible, the democratic nations must arrive at a "Declaration
of Inter-dependence," which must become the new Magna
Carta of humanity.

In this Declaration of Inter-dependence we must clearly
set forth certain elementary principles of social, political
and economic life which each nation has to accept and
adopt. We must clearly state that violation of any one of
these rules and principles will bring immediate action by a
collective body of other nations or any other collective international organization.

Such a change in the international life, the regulation of
national independence, had been clearly foreseen by the

signatories of the Declaration of Independence in 1776. It says: "That whenever any Form of Government becomes destructive of these ends (Life, Liberty and the Pursuit of Happiness) it is the Right of the People to alter or to abolish it, and to institute new Government, laying its foundation on such principles and organizing its powers in such form, as to them shall seem most likely to effect their Safety and Happiness."

This most unsafe and unhappy period in history, this catastrophe in which we find ourselves makes it imperative that we listen to the advice of the Fathers of Independence and tackle the problem at its root.

# XIII

# *Force*

FOR TWO CENTURIES the German peoples, whether under the leadership of Frederick the Great, Prince Bismarck, Kaiser Wilhelm II, or Adolf Hitler, have acted according to the Germanic conception of international law—"Might is right." This doctrine has been worked out by German philosophers and invariably practised by German statesmen during the past generations.

The doctrine was categorically denied by the democratic nations who always regarded it as a most immoral principle.

The opposition to the theory, "Might is right," led the democratic nations so far away from it that their conception of an international life was more or less exemplified by a principle which could be formulated as "Right is might" or "Right without might."

Their aversion to might as the basis of international life was so strong that they *denied* might and strove to abolish violence and force in all forms.

It is difficult to say which doctrine—the doctrine of "Might is right," or the strange doctrine of ignoring force— is more responsible for the present world situation.

We always thought that might, violence, force were identical with war, and the preservation of peace meant only one thing: avoiding the use of force. Dozens of examples could be cited in history proving that freedom-loving nations have been attacked and destroyed because they did not believe in force and thought any solution was preferable to the use of force.

When the League of Nations was founded after the First World War, the cardinal problem was whether force should be at the disposal of the League. All pacifists were against this and the League was instituted without any provision for the use of force to meet the demands of necessity. That meant that from the very beginning of its existence, the League was functioning in a vacuum of unreality, without any chance of settling such matters which could not have been equally well settled without its existence.

It was with the utmost tenacity and determination that the governments refused to permit the League to apply force. There were at least ten occasions during 1931 and 1939 when the slightest manifestation of force behind the resolutions of the League could have prevented the present world war. Through the most extraordinary acrobatics of reasoning, somehow this was always blocked. And when for the first time that unrealistic machinery of Geneva was put to the test, when more than fifty nations angrily voted for the application of sanctions against Italy, the leading democratic statesmen declared to the world that sanctions must be kept harmless; otherwise Europe would be plunged into war.

There were enough sanctions adopted to irritate the aggressor power, but under no conditions were such sanctions advocated, the application of which would involve force. Sir Samuel Hoare said: "There may be degrees of aggression. Elasticity is part of security." And when in order to "preserve peace" the democratic governments favored the recognition of the Italian conquest of Ethiopia, Lord Halifax said: "Great as is the League of Nations, the ends it exists to serve are greater than itself, and the greatest of those ends is peace."

The peace was so perfectly preserved and the aggressor power was so grateful to the democratic nations for not applying sanctions against it that in less than four years Italy declared war against Great Britain and France.

All these sad experiences should make clear to us what we ought to have known without any experience, that force cannot be denied or ignored.

*Force is a reality.*

If there is one law which can be deduced from the history of mankind, it is that whenever and wherever force was not used in the service of the law, it was used against the law.

It is pure gangsterism that we are fighting today. This fact more than anything paralyzed the judgment of our democratic statesmen during the past ten years. We have been accustomed to regard ministers, ambassadors and representatives of other nations as gentlemen, people similar in background and education to our own leaders.

We have seen gangsters organizing bank robberies, bootlegging, the kidnapping of children, the making and circulating of counterfeit money, but we have never before seen and could never imagine that a band of gangsters could take possession of the entire machinery of a state and could organize and run a great state entirely on gangster principles and methods. Our democratic politicians and diplomats have been helpless in the face of politicians and diplomats who had the same impulses and motives, and who had the same conception about society, convention and decency as common-law gangsters. And yet that is exactly what has happened.

But why did it happen? And how could it happen? The answer lies in the fact that we despised force, we misunderstood force, we excluded force as an instrument of democratic policy. So the enemies of democracy used force—nothing but force!

We did not want law with force; just rules with goodwill. So now we have to reckon with force without law.

As long as we identify force and the use of force with war, and believe that peace is merely a period without the use of force, we shall never have peace and will always be the victims of force.

We cannot deny the existence of rain just because there are days of sunshine; and we cannot deny that there is night just because it is not dark at noontime.

Force is a reality that exists. We cannot deny it. We cannot call "peace" just those short intervals when by chance nobody happens to be using force. In any period when violence does not manifest itself, we can, under present conditions, be certain that force *will* reappear.

Only if we *use* force, if we clearly decide *when* it should be applied, and if in all such cases we see that it *is* applied, is there any chance that force and violence will not be used against our institutions, our freedom and our lives.

Only if we put force in the service of justice can we hope that it will not be used against justice. Only if we use force to maintain peace can we hope that it will not be used against peace.

The criterion of every organized form of social life is that a superior authority has the legal right to employ force in order to prevent the individual members of society from using force.

The only way to defeat the doctrine of "Might is right," is not "Right without might," but "Right *based* on might."

Institutions must be created in advance with the purpose that might will be applied to the limit whenever and wherever right is in danger. As Saint Simon said: "Every reunion of peoples, just as every reunion of men, needs common institutions, needs an organization. Outside of this, everything is decided by sheer force."

In any kind of planning for the future, on whatever basis we want to organize the relationship among peoples, the condition of success is the rehabilitation of force, its recognition as an indispensable reality, its inclusion in our future scheme of organization, and its independent use in cases specified in advance and in forms instituted in advance.

That Christianity survived twenty centuries and exists today, we have to thank not only the Apostles and the Saints, but in equal measure the zeal of the crusaders.

The time has come when the survival of democracy needs no more Apostles, but crusaders who are convinced that peace is unimaginable in any form, unless it is based on force.

# XIV

# *Aggression*

To MAKE THE NATIONS SAFE from aggression has been for the past twenty years one of the most popular slogans of democratic diplomacy. We had established a status quo and said that no changes could be made unless they were based on mutual understanding of all the parties concerned. We had "outlawed" war and said that the use of armed forces in order to achieve a change in the status quo without the consent of the other party is "aggression." We preached that aggression was a crime and tried to unite all the other nations (at least within the framework of the League of Nations) to take up arms on the side of the victim of aggression. As under the given circumstances there was no chance of any change in the status quo by agreements, "aggressions" started within a few years after the establishment of this artificial world construction.

For many years, particularly during the meetings of the ill-fated Disarmament Conference, there was widespread scholastic debate in order to obtain a "definition of aggression." None of the many definitions brought forth was unanimously accepted, but all those attempts to get a definition of aggression had as a basis the idea that the nation which for the first time crosses the territorial boundaries of another nation with armed forces is the aggressor.

This conception about aggression is most unsatisfactory and creates not only complete confusion about the real origin and beginning of aggression, but also paralyzes the freedom-loving and democratic nations and exposes them to the greatest dangers.

Is aggression a crime? And if so, why?

Aggression is undoubtedly that kind of human activity which in many instances during our history has brought positive results, has spurred progress and helped to spread civilization and culture.

The prototype of acts of aggression is the activity of the missionaries. To penetrate without invitation and mutual consent into remote continents with the intention to change entirely the way of living of strange people is indeed an act of aggression. But is it a crime, and is it to be disapproved?

The Crusades were an act of aggression. The French Revolution and America's conquest of the West were acts of aggression. But can we by any means disapprove these events and call them illegal or a crime?

It appears obvious that the conception according to which the beginning of the use of force is the only form of aggression, and that it is in all cases aggression, could only be right in an absolutely perfect and just world order, which has never existed, and almost certainly never will exist in our world of constant changes and evolutions. It is indefensible to call aggression any kind of forceful act independent of whether it is directed against an innocent people or against an injustice.

The idea expressed by a leader of the French Revolution, "Where there is order and injustice, disorder is the beginning of justice," is also valid in international relations. The first use of armed forces can, therefore, by no means be a satisfactory criterion for the term "aggression."

If a nation attacks one of our naval bases or airdromes, we call it "aggression," and we are prepared to go to war in order to defend our possessions. But when our enemies attack the principles on which our entire life is based, our freedom, our families, our prosperity, and our future, we are indifferent and fail to arrive at the point of calling it "aggression" and to react accordingly.

England and France declared war when their ally Poland was overrun by the German armed forces. The United States declared war when the Japanese bombed American possessions in Hawaii and in the Philippines. This was fully in accordance with our established policies that war is outlawed, that aggression is a crime, and that aggression is the first military action, and only military action.

It is almost incalculable how many lives and how much wealth and destruction this conception will cost us.

The march of the German armies and the dive-bombing by the Japanese air forces were the $n$th act of aggression against the democratic powers. To call just this $n$th act "aggression" because it was accompanied by the fireworks of gun powder explosions is indeed most unsatisfactory.

This war started when Benito Mussolini proclaimed publicly and solemnly that Fascist Italy's aim is to destroy the principles of the French Revolution, and when Adolf Hitler's government proclaimed publicly and solemnly that for

Nazi Germany "Right is what is in the interest of the German Volk."

It was in that moment, if our democracies were working according to present-day realities, and had we had a clear vision of the real possessions we must defend, that the aroused forces of the free peoples ought to have intervened to stop this aggression.

The defense of our way of life, the defense of our nations and the destruction of the aggressive forces would have cost at that time less than one thousandth in blood, sweat, toil and tears of what it will cost now.

In the face of this reality, it is impossible to say that such questions as, "What is aggression?" "Where does it begin?" "When must we start fighting in order to stop it?" are merely theoretical. In fact, on the correct reply to such questions and on the correct interpretation of such theoretical principles rest the life and death of millions of men, and the preservation or waste of hundreds of billions of dollars.

The second great danger of the superficial interpretation of aggression—calling it merely armed intervention—is the negative, defensive mentality which it involves and which it spreads among the freedom-loving nations.

War being outlawed, military initiative being aggression, and aggression being a crime, the democratic nations have been lulled into a negative conception of life which can only hasten their destruction.

We have been teaching in our schools, in our parliaments, in our press and in our various religious and political associations, a kind of pacifism which is as remote from the realities of the world and from the real conception of peace as incantation is from medical science. We refuse to recognize biological facts by simply not mentioning them by their names, and we try to cure our illnesses with pious preachings, stubbornly refusing to listen to scientifically trained physicians and to follow their advice.

This strange conception of peace and our equally unreal conception of aggression created a passive, negative conception of life among democratic nations which involved all the manifestations of our existence. We wanted nothing. We had absolutely no intentions, no ideals, no purpose, except to keep at peace, keep shooting away from us, and to keep intact those little earthly possessions we inherited. This ignorance of the most elementary forces of this world made us incapable not only of preventing certain events, but even of coping with them when they occurred.

An extraordinary spectacle was that series of fights by which Nazi Germany defeated one by one all the European nations. No nation had possessed the mental capacity to understand what was going on and to prevent its steady progress. This would have meant initiative, action, prevention—all made impossible through our negative conception of life.

The life of an individual, just like the life of a nation, is nothing but constant action, initiative and struggle. Whoever stops is defeated and must cede his place to others. There is no such thing as holding one's position in this continuing progress and in trying to force others to stop, too. A conception of static peace is inconceivable, and if we do not put the dynamic forces of life into the service of our cause, they will be used by others and directed against us.

We can only prevent these dynamic forces from leading to wars if we are prepared to steer them into lawful channels. But we shall certainly not be able to stop them by the simple expedient of ignoring them and by trying individually to escape from them.

The successes of Hitler can in a certain degree be explained by the right analysis of the effects of these two drives. In a world ruled almost entirely by statesmen, diplomats and civil servants completely submerged in a static, negative conception and rendered totally impotent to act and to take any initiative, there suddenly arose an uneducated outlaw, with no knowledge whatsoever of international affairs, of diplomacy, of private or constitutional law, but merely possessing the simple faculty of a primitive man *to act*. Having no control over this primitive impulse, like our over-educated, over-cautious statesmen have, he had always on his side the power of "events," which is a thousand times stronger than the power of arguments.

If we want to learn from the past twenty years and to prevent the repetition of such catastrophes, we must begin by changing this sterile and passive attitude of our peoples. We must realize that on the battlefield defensive measures may sometimes be a strategic necessity; in the field of ideas, it is always identical with defeat.

It is utterly unsatisfactory to teach our youth and to proclaim to our public that democracy is the best form of government, that ours is a just cause and that the forces of evil will be destroyed because ultimately the righteous cause must always prevail. Such a fatalistic attitude is really a weak defense of our shortcomings. It is correct to say that the righteous cause usually prevails, but we can trace in history periods in which the "righteous" cause suffered defeat for generations and even for centuries.

The more active and the more positive, not the more righteous, will win this fight between the democratic and the totalitarian forces. Righteousness is a factor in victory only insofar as it gives us more faith and more force to be active and positive.

Our primary effort must be, therefore, to pull out from our public life the roots of these static conceptions of defense. We must clearly state those democratic principles in the national and international life which we want to preserve, those principles which we want to establish and for which we are willing to fight. We must give these principles a realistic and understandable interpretation which would make possible their existence and their defense.

We must declare as aggression any attack on these principles, whether the attack is military or ideological. And all nations which champion these principles must in such cases regard themselves as being the objects of aggression, whether the attack is military or ideological.

Only when we can clearly detect the origin of the aggression against our way of life, and only if we possess the mechanism of suppressing any such attacks, shall we have created a state of affairs which we might call safe from aggression. In any international life organized on that basis, military acts and "shooting war" will be reduced to a minimum, and when it does occur it will meet with the same overwhelming might as a common criminal finds in a well-organized city.

# XV

# *Preventive War*

"You CANNOT make peace through war."

This is one of the most dangerous sophisms with which the 100-per-cent pacifists have indoctrinated their propaganda against the use of force, against the application of sanctions, against any kind of action which might have prevented the outbreak of this world war.

Even if we call the application of force "war," it must be said that *only* such application of force can preserve peace.

What is the difference between such an application of force advocated here and wars as we have known them heretofore?

The answer is very simple: The existence of law.

Though one of the first commandments of Christianity is "Thou shalt not kill," the Church, when it had sovereignty to do so, condemned to death and executed thousands of individuals who had violated the laws. And since the existence of the nation-states, even in the most Christian and the most democratic ones, the application of force —execution, imprisonment and other forms of punishment—has been the only possible safeguard of Christian or democratic principles in human society.

There is no contradiction in that. And we must constantly keep in mind the development of our social organization if we sincerely want to find a solution to our present-day problem: the organization of international society.

The fact that there is no coercive international law creates a situation in which criminals, determined to act, enjoy all the liberties and all the advantages of lawlessness. In the present situation, simply because the repression or the prevention of a crime is not the result of the application of a law, of a judgment, of a punishment, it appears to us equally as a crime.

In fact, it is. Any punishment without law is equal to crime. Only the existence of law creates the difference between crime and justice.

It is, therefore, of primary importance that the principle of *legal war* as an instrument of democratic policy should be established. Only through the institution of legal wars shall we ever be able to preserve peace and never through alliances, or through such Utopian documents as the Covenant of the League or the Kellogg Pact.

The most important form of legal wars to be established is the *preventive war*. Just as in social life preventive measures are more human and more effective; just as the trend in modern medicine is to prevent diseases and not only to cure them, in international affairs we must try to prevent major armed clashes and not wait until the outbreak of hostilities is inevitable.

Until now the idea of preventive war has been taboo in democratic nations. Whenever in the democratic countries public opinion was aroused against the step-by-step preparation for this war by the totalitarians, the Fascist propagandists shouted that the democracies *wanted* a preventive war, because naturally they would not stop acting as they did unless the democracies applied force. And this was sufficient argument to disarm the will of resistance in the democracies and to give to the "appeasers" power to arrange matters with the enemies of democracy: to capitulate rather than to fight.

Never was a war more unnecessary and easier to prevent than the war we have to suffer today. It was clear to every man with the senses to see and hear and understand that the totalitarian conceptions were aiming at the destruction of the democratic powers and at the domination of the world. Nothing would have been easier to prevent the growing might of our enemies than the undertaking of a preventive operation which, until 1938, would have been insignificant.

It is beyond discussion that the policy of the democratic powers, to wait passively until the moment when this world war became inevitable, was a false policy. But it is useless to reproach democratic governments for this disastrous policy. They acted in the only way in which they were authorized to act according to the established constitutions, laws and principles of their countries.

Whether we shall ever be able to organize human society in such a way that wars will be made impossible, and that "eternal peace" will reign over this planet, is impossible to tell. Most probably it will never be possible to attain this ideal. We must be more modest and more realistic if we want to attain at least something, and take the next step in

the direction of this ideal. And this next step is the prevention of world wars on the scale and with the destructive
power of the 1914-18 World War and the present one.

This can only be done through the institution and legalization of preventive wars, as common democratic action
against the growth and spreading of anti-democratic destructive forces which must and will always lead into illegal
wars.

Without such institution of law, it will never be possible
to make democratic nations aware of the seriousness of a
situation until it is too late. To ordinary people, the appeal
for inaction is always much stronger than the appeal for
action. There will always be an overwhelming majority
in critical times who in democratic countries will say: "It
is none of our business"; "Let us keep out of it"; "Let us
concentrate on the defense of our own country and to hell
with the others." And those who instinctively would urge
action and prevention will always be called "warmongers,"
in spite of the fact that action might prevent a major war,
whereas inaction will certainly bring war.

Once we have established such an organization, we shall
probably have two or three wars in a century, but they will
be infinitesimally smaller in character, their devastation and
destructive power will be incomparably less, and the relationship between those legal wars to the present and past
wars will be the same as the relationship is between the
killings among cannibal tribes and the murder cases in a
modern civilized state.

The mere institution of preventive war as a legal instrument of international policy, the mere threat of it, would

prevent wars in nine cases out of ten, and make the use of this instrument unnecessary.

The only kind of peace conceivable on this globe and in the present century is the establishment of certain primary rules among peoples and the institution of armed forces to intervene automatically and unconditionally in any part of the world wherever these rules are violated. Such a revolutionary change can never be brought about without the full recognition of the out-dated order which only catastrophes like the present world war can reveal. We must hope that this war will bring the truth of the character and relationship of peace and war, and of the problems connected with them, to the minds of the masses, and that a clear vision of a better future will be shaped during this war, while the butchery and the misery last. If we miss that chance, generations may have to wait for another.

Justice started on this earth with the first public execution of a criminal based on judgment.

Peace will start on this earth on the day when for the first time a group of nations will wage war, based on previously accepted principles, against a violator of international law.

# XVI

## *Utopia*

THESE PAGES do not contain one single new idea. It is hardly possible to bring out any really new and original idea with regard to the political and social organization of the world. And certainly there is no need for any new idea to solve our present international problems.

The principles of good government have been discovered centuries ago. The basic ideas concerning human society, worked out by Confucius, Plato, Aristotle, and more explicitly by the philosophers of the eighteenth century, can be regarded as axiomatic. The only problem is their proper interpretation, their constant evolution, their harmonization with present-day realities, and their application through such institutions as may give them the greatest force and the best expression.

All major conflicts, all revolutions and all wars have had their origin in the fact that the existing institutions, the prevailing interpretation of principles and methods of political procedure have been in conflict with the ever-changing realities. To believe, at any time, that the already existing form is important, and not the content, must and always will lead to catastrophes.

The tragedy of mankind is that, as Goethe said, no generation is living under the laws of their own time. We always have to carry the weight of laws, institutions, rules and habits established by our forefathers in order to express properly and adequately certain principles in their time, which in the existing form do not express those ideals any more today.

The reluctance to admit the necessity of changes is deep-rooted in human nature. Most people take the attitude that discussion of political changes is premature—until it has become outdated. They used to call any planning for the future, any foresight and clear vision of coming changes, "Utopian."

They do not realize that the criterion of Utopia is always the attempt to organize the present or future according to the image of the past. All those dreamers of past centuries, whom we today call Utopians, were longing for a future of pastoral atmosphere. Each preached some kind of a "return to nature."

Those who only want to "defend" and "conserve" do not realize that in fact they, themselves, are Utopians because they believe in the possibility of maintaining everlastingly certain forms and institutions without adapting them to the constant changes of this world.

So we see today a man who wants to re-establish the old Roman Empire of 2,000 years ago. Another man dreams of the restoration of the Holy Roman Empire of the German Nation, dead for so many centuries. And these men pretend to be the leaders of the youth, the prophets of the future, the creators of a new order. They dare to condemn the ideals of democracy and individual freedom hardly 150 years in existence, as being worn out and outdated.

Not only the antediluvian dictatorships, but also the democratic peoples are governed today by Utopians of the highest degree, by men who worship "nation" and "race," who believe themselves capable of creating a League of Nations composed of sovereign national states, who believe in the production of wealth by tariff walls and autarchy, who do not want to "meddle" in the internal affairs of other states, who want to live "isolated" and to be "left alone."

They try to persuade us that the application of democratic ideas in the conduct of international affairs has failed, that free trade has failed, that the League of Nations has failed, that the Naval and Kellogg Pacts have failed, and that, therefore, there is no chance of getting democratic principles accepted in international relations. And they conclude that we must limit democracy in domestic affairs and reduce to a minimum contact with the foreign world.

It is ridiculous to pretend that because the first attempt in history to organize international life on a democratic basis has failed, because the Covenant of the League and other conventions have been violated, the principles which they attempted to express proved to be wrong and consequently must be abolished.

At the beginning of human civilization a few primitive rules were formed, which were regarded as the *conditio sine qua non* of any social life and which were called the Ten Commandments. For twenty centuries the most powerful organizations represented by the Church and the States have done their utmost to get these primitive principles of the Ten Commandments universally respected. In order to put this aim into effect, the States and the Church had at their disposal such means as the scaffold, the police, the anathema, the armies, the devil, prison and hell. In spite of all these manifold material and spiritual measures of enforcement, and after twenty centuries, not one day passes in the most highly civilized and most Christian countries in the world when murder, theft and adultery do not occur.

Is there anyone who would claim that because there are still murderers and thieves after so many centuries of effort to do away with them, the Ten Commandments have proved to be worthless, inapplicable, and should, therefore, be abolished?

But there are people in great number who pretend to be statesmen and who seriously say that because the first attempt in human history to organize international life along certain principles has failed, these principles are inapplicable, ineffectual and must be abandoned.

Today hardly a piece of political writing appears which does not start with the following phrases: "Technical development renders the world always smaller and smaller. Distances disappear, and men and peoples are living closer and closer to each other. This development of the technique makes tariff walls, national antagonisms and wars an anachronism, and will automatically make the waging of wars impossible."

This conclusion is a half truth. That the evolution of the technique brings people and continents closer to each other is correct, but such a geographical and physical "rapprochement" may have two consequences: (1) A political and economic rapprochement, or (2) Fights and quarrels more devastating than ever, precisely because of the proximity of men to each other. Which one of these two possibilities will occur depends on matters essentially non-technical.

Another reason why the changes through which we are going are so painful is the fact that the pioneer period in industrialism is over. It is no longer a great personal achievement to produce textiles or to build railroads. A hundred, or even fifty years ago, these undertakings required great personal risks, daring personal initiative, inventiveness, courage and determination to fight. But today industrial activity has become a more or less routine, administrative work.

We have seen Russia building in twenty years an industrial organization which took England, the United States and Germany more than a century to build up. This "miracle" will certainly shortly be repeated in India and in China. We cannot stop this evolution and cannot endeavor to keep industrial power concentrated in the hands of certain individuals, certain corporations or certain nations by artificial means. Such an attempt would almost certainly lead to explosions.

The static conception of the maintenance of a status quo —any status quo—and the primitive instincts of those nations which are not satisfied with a given status quo—and there will always be such unsatisfied nations—to make changes by force are not two different policies, but the two sides of one and the same political conception.

Both are false. Both policies must lead from one war to

another, because they do nothing but perpetuate a trend which has been followed by humanity since time immemorial.

In planning a better immediate future, it is of the utmost importance to prevent the formation of such rigid constructions which in one or two generations might become just as reactionary and antiquated as most of our present institutions are.

Those who have given up the ideals of economic freedom have been propagating for some time planned economy controlled by the state. Through such various national, planned economies, economic competition and anarchy became only worse than ever because the sovereign units taking part in this competition are much more powerful than the single individuals were. It is quite obvious that no economic problem can satisfactorily be solved if the planning will remain the sovereign authority of *many* national governments.

It is even more important to prevent the formation of such rigid political constructions which would only aggravate and enlarge the conflicts to come. As stepping stones, regional solutions might be indispensable, but it would be dangerous to believe that such solutions as Pan-Europa or Pan-Asia or Pan-America would solve our international problems for more than a very short time.

What might happen, in the hypothesis that we could organize the world in five or six such large political units without changing the fundamental principles of international relationship, we can clearly see in the works of the champion of the Pan-Europa Movement.

Count Coudenhove-Kalergi in his book, *Europe Awakes,*[1] writes the following: "Europe must under all conditions decline to become the policeman of the world. An international army or air force that would embrace also the other continents would menace European peace more than it would safeguard it. The Chinese question might lead in the next years and decades to the greatest conflicts in East Asia, which Europe cannot prevent, but in which Europe would be dragged, if it does not remain strictly neutral. . . . Pan-Europa demands a European army for the defense of Europe and for the security of the European peace, but it rejects a League army which would not secure this peace, but which would threaten it."

This is the verbatim repetition of the arguments of the most ardent isolationists, non-interventionists and neutralists, with the one difference that it is claimed in the name of a territory somewhat larger than France or Germany or Spain, but smaller than the United States, Brazil or Russia. It is difficult to see why a Pan-European policy of non-intervention in China would be wiser than the Anglo-French policy of non-intervention was in Spain; why a strictly Pan-European army would better defend Europe than the strictly American army was able to prevent an attack on the United States and why the "strict neutrality" of Pan-Europa in a prospective Far Eastern conflict would be a higher moral attitude, from the point of view of international life, than the "neutrality" of France and England was in the Czechoslovakian crisis.

There is no salvation whatsoever in huge political struc-

[1] Coudenhove-Kalergi: *Europa Erwacht,* page 178.

tures without a clarification and an unmistakable interpretation of those primary principles on which *any* form of international order has to be based.

The disregard of this elementary necessity was also the reason for the failure of the League of Nations. The Covenant was an essentially international document, but its signatories were the sovereign national states. In the League of Nations building there was an international atmosphere. The League was a sort of an aristocratic club where periodically the same few hundred statesmen and the same few hundred newspapermen met. It was an excellent thing that they had a place of meeting, that they could exchange their views. But nothing was changed at home. In each country the entire education continued to be nationalistic. The press remained nationalistic. The administration and government remained nationalistic.

It was a naive Utopia to believe that the representatives and the functionaries of such nationalistic states could by meeting periodically create a better international understanding. It was like starting the construction of a new building with the roof. There is but one way to build, and that is to start at the foundation, even if constructing that way means longer work.

To distinguish the possible from the impossible, to distinguish reality from Utopia, is essential in politics. Utopia can never be characterized by its substance. The two characteristics of any conception of Utopia are (1) the wish to project the past into the future; (2) the belief that technical developments might make human nature better and kinder.

We still are a long way from knowing the exact scientific

mechanism of the social and the economic life. But the experiments of the past twenty years prove sufficiently that politics is not far removed from mathematics, and that we have no justification whatsoever to expect that if we try long enough we might obtain five by adding two and two.

# XVII

## *Principles and Institutions*

WE MUST ALWAYS bear in mind that any theoretical systems of human society are not only unrealizable and have never existed, but *in toto* represent an impossibility, a state of affairs in which it would be unbearable to live. Real life at any moment in history has always been "a period of transition," having many elements of various past systems. No radical change, no revolution has ever been able to achieve more than a part of its program of which life has made a synthesis with many elements of the past.

What is required is not a detailed and in itself closed system of the future, but a clear understanding of the basic principles which show us the road leading in the right direction.

Whether the next step will be a new League of Nations, regional groupings, continental organizations, a union of the English-speaking world, or a world government, is of secondary importance. The essential fact is that we understand what the principles of democracy mean in twentieth-century terms, and that on their basis the process of *international integration* should start.

Following that natural evolution any one of the above-mentioned constructions would help us a great step forward.

In some kind of an international charter we have to re-state the principles of the Magna Carta, the Declaration of Independence, the Bill of Rights and the Declaration of the Rights of Man and of the Citizen. What are those basic principles of democracy? And what is their meaning in the middle of the twentieth century?

*First:* The right of freedom. In the original documents it was clearly defined that freedom consists in the "power of doing whatever does not injure the freedom of another." Translated in the international field, this means that every nation must be free and independent, but only insofar as the power of exercising this right does not injure the freedom and independence of other nations. At present these limitations of national independence and national freedom are non-existent and are not defined, and without such definition, the freedom and independence of the nations are meaningless. They only lead to wars.

*Second:* According to the original charters of democracy, equality means that a law must be applied in equal measure to every individual, whether it protects a man or punishes him. Translated in the international field today, this principle means that every nation must be equal under the law. As the world is organized today, there is no international law whatsoever, and without such a law "equality" of nations is meaningless, and only leads to wars.

*Third:* The original charters of democracy guarantee to each man the right of security, and state that security results from the co-operation of all to secure the rights of each. This means with respect to international application that the security of each nation can result only from the collaboration of all the other nations to secure the rights of each one of them. This definition clearly outlaws conceptions like neutrality or non-intervention, which can never assure security to any nation, and which are contrary to the essence of the basic charters of democratic principles. We have seen how the disregard of the original conception of security, how neutrality and non-intervention led each nation which believed in them to wars and destruction.

*Fourth:* In the original charters of democracy, it is stated that sovereignty resides essentially in the community—in the universality of the citizens. They explicitly state that no individual and no group of individuals can exercise sovereign authority. As the world is organized today, it is obvious that sovereignty does not reside in the universality of citizens, but that contrary to the spirit of the original charters of democracy sovereign rights are exercised by groups of individuals we call "States."

The existence of some hundred sovereign states exercising sovereign authority is in total contradiction to the democratic conception of sovereignty which must rest in the community. It is, therefore, imperative to carry out the separation of powers in this field, to give back to the community absolute sovereignty and to give individual nations and individual states only such sovereign authority which has its source in universal sovereignty.

These are the first steps towards a constitutional life in world affairs. The Declaration of the Rights of Man and of the Citizen says: "Any society in which the guarantee of the rights is not secured or the separation of powers not determined has no constitution at all."

As to the duties of the individual nations towards each other and to the community, this was also clearly expressed in the great democratic charters by the thought that anyone who violates the law declares himself to be in a state of war with society.

These principles must be made clear and be codified *now,* during this war. They must be written in gold letters on our flags; they must become the soul of our soldiers; they must be on all wave lengths.

Our victory must be the victory of these new principles on the basis of which we can build a new and better world society. These principles and the promise of a way of life they hold out to us are our most powerful weapon. It is the only weapon that can give sufficient fire power to our bombers, tanks and warships.

The proclamation of these principles cannot be postponed, to be discussed *after* victory. They are the wings, they are the only historical justification of our coming victory.

Always in history, great revolutionary changes take place during wars. We must mold the amorphous masses on the five continents now, before they become rigid again in a form contrary to our ideas.

We must act now, during the present war, because no military victory can give us the guarantee that it will create a reasonable world. Only a political victory can do that.

And we can never have political victory without waging a political war simultaneously with the military war.

It was one of the great tragedies of our time that the demo-.cratic nations and the democratic governments did not grasp—and still do not grasp—the fact that a gigantic political struggle is going on, of which the military war is merely one symptom.

We have to lead mankind according to historical necessities or we shall lose the leadership. We are now in the midst of a political and social revolution of which the international war is only one part. We must be crusaders of new ideas. We must not continue to be defenders of futile past systems, the re-establishment of which has always been proved throughout history to be Utopian.

The abolition of international and economic particularism is a historical necessity. The restriction of national sovereignties and the beginning of the process of international integration will be the result of this war.

This development can take place in two forms: either by mutual agreement between the hitherto independent and sovereign nations or through forceful imposition.

Should the new democratic order have to be created by compulsion—and according to historical precedents it most probably will—then it is essential that the Anglo-American nations should undertake the task. They must undertake it not only because on the proper reorganization of the world will depend the survival of their own democratic institutions and the very existence of their peoples, but also because the past few centuries have proved that in the present phase of human history Anglo-American supremacy means general progress for all mankind, whereas all attempts at domination by any of the other potential world powers always meant reaction to the democratic evolution.

The democratic nations must be aroused from their static and defensive conceptions and become imbued with the dynamic spirit of attack and conquest. Only ideals and principles can achieve this.

We shall not have victory if we want only to be left alone and to defend what we possess. If the democratic peoples really value their principles, cherish their freedom, and are attached to their way of life, they cannot accept or tolerate the establishment in their neighborhood of political and social conceptions representing the complete negation of their own principles. They must have the iron will to spread their ideas all over the world and to fight the enemies of their conceptions and ideals wherever they may be. We cannot win this war for democracy without convictions.

And there is only one criterion of real conviction—the will to spread it.

If we enforce the laws guaranteeing freedom of man everywhere, and make clear what these freedoms are, providing in the same laws for the limitations and the defense of this freedom; if we can make clear through what limitations we can obtain real freedom of speech, freedom of the press and freedom of assembly; if we enforce the principles of international relationship which are identical with the principles of relationship between individuals in a democratic state; if we proclaim the inter-dependence of nations, limiting national sovereignty, outlawing neutrality and creating an organization having the force to safeguard these principles, to prosecute and punish any nation violating the established laws and principles—then it will be of small importance what external forms nations or groups of nations adopt.

Our aim should not be to abolish variety and diversity in this world. The cultural and traditional varieties existing between the different nations are the greatest charm of our existence. Our aim must be merely to stop these varieties from degenerating to armed conflicts, to guide the eternal struggle for life into more civilized channels and to create a political order that will at last make possible the solution of the economic and social problems of *our* age.

It looks as if political unity were the only possibility of maintaining and safeguarding cultural diversity.

The outcome of this war and the shape of things in the coming century will in a large measure depend upon by whom and under what conditions these foundations of a rejuvenated democratic world will be laid. A great handicap for the peaceful and freedom-loving nations is that today they are led by a ruling class completely devoid of vision, talent, will power and capacity for action. It is most doubtful whether those people who have lost the peace and appear to be incapable of understanding the real significance and character of this world war will be able to create a new world order superior to the past.

The selection of leaders is an essential problem of any democratic organization. As this intricate machinery is operating today, it appears that the quality of statesmanship, vision, wise leadership, self-sacrifice and capacity for action are qualities essentially different from the qualities required to obtain power.

The question of personnel is a tremendously important one, as man is the beginning and the end of social life, and finally every idea, institution, and administrative office is represented by men. Since the beginning of democratic societies, the ideal was that the most capable man, regardless of rank, wealth and origin, should find his way to the top. The general ballot was supposed to be the right road leading to this goal.

If we examine the records of those people who came to power this way, and who had an influential voice in shaping public affairs during the past years, we might reasonably doubt whether the present method of obtaining nomination and election to legislative bodies and governments is sufficiently selective to guarantee the best possible leadership. There are too many cases in which it soon became apparent that those entrusted with the responsibility of formulating and directing our affairs were lacking in the elementary knowledge of the problems to be dealt with, and did not possess the basic qualities of leadership.

In every other field of human activity, a certain capacity for reasoning and a certain elementary knowledge of facts are requisite for any advancement. Among astronomers, there may be hundreds of different views relative to the construction of the universe. All these divergent views must be freely and thoroughly discussed by scientists in universities and academies. Only through such free discussion can the true and accurate theory be adopted, and the proper authorities be determined. But should anyone in such discussions assert and persist in the thought that the earth is not a globe, but a flat plate surrounded by water, and that it is not revolving around the sun, but that the sun is revolving around the earth, he would not be allowed to teach in universities, he would not get academic awards, and he would certainly not be considered a scientific authority.

Nobody would feel that barring such an obviously unqualified person from a professorship in a university was against freedom of science and anti-democratic. It is simply an accepted fact that discussion, which must ever be kept free for the sake of scientific truth and progress, has gone beyond the point to which he sticks and which he teaches, and that nobody holding such views can be taken seriously.

There are thousands of problems concerning the constitution of the human body, and these problems must be freely discussed in all medical circles. Every opinion must be expressed and must be studied with the utmost care and attention. Only thus can the best minds in medical science come to the foreground and constructively help to fight disease. But if in such medical discussions someone would contend and stoutly defend his contention that there is no such thing as blood circulation in the human body, nobody in any assembly of medical science would listen to him. He would quite naturally be looked upon as an ignoramus. And he would vainly insist upon being allowed to be a professor of medicine on the ground that freedom of speech and freedom of science give him the right to teach these views.

These principles of selection are universal in all fields of human endeavor, except in the political field.

Here, though the problems which have to be dealt with

are the most complicated, and vitally affect the very lives of hundreds of millions, we still listen to people who believe that notions like neutrality, isolation, non-intervention, etc., etc., could be the subject of serious public discussion. They are just as dead conceptions as the views about the globe before Copernicus and the theories about blood before Harvey.

We must correct our present system of selecting representatives and government, and must require that whoever we send to a legislative assembly should possess not only a colorful personality, influential friends and rhetorical talents, but also a certain minimum knowledge of public affairs and of democratic principles.

To correct and to limit in such a way our present system of free election would not only not infringe upon the democratic principle of free voting, but would give a far better opportunity to the people to exercise their democratic right of election by entrusting representation to such people who really do represent democratic ideas.

It cannot be the criterion of democracy that a man with anti-democratic ideas should have the possibility of getting elected. Only men with the right conception of the modern world and with the sufficiently deep-rooted democratic convictions can lead us to the next step: to the foundation of a democratic international life.

Skeptics will obviously ask who will be the judge, who will guarantee that such limitations of freedom of speech, of freedom of assembly, of freedom of the press will not be abused. And who will be the judge that the men to be elected possess the required qualifications for democratic leadership. The answer is simple:

Abuses will naturally occur from time to time, as there is no conceivable organization of society perfect in an absolute sense.

In many cases the only possible way to cure a deadly disease is by applying therapeutic measures which, while overcoming the malady, more or less react on other organs of the body which are not affected by the disease. Nevertheless, this is the only acknowledged method of treatment and is not challenged by any authority. Nor does anyone challenge the urgent necessity of surgical operations in spite of the full knowledge of the risks they might involve.

We have come to the conclusion that the present interpretation of democratic principles, and certain democratic institutions as they function today, are a deadly danger to democracy itself, and have been the direct cause of the destruction of democracy in the majority of countries. Having made the proper diagnosis, we have to undertake the necessary drastic measures and reforms, even, if by saving the very existence of democracy, we carry certain unavoidable risks.

But there is no reason to fear that such abuses would be of any importance. Once the proper democratic legislation —national and international—is enacted, there is no justification at all to believe that independent courts will fail to handle situations properly and in a democratic sense.

Whether "wars" in general can ever be abolished is impossible to tell. Probably it will never be the case. But this type of wars—wars between nations separated from each other by artificial boundaries—can be abolished as soon as certain parts of the sovereignty exercised today by these nations are transferred to a higher organ. Religious wars were stopped only when the nations began to exercise the sovereign rights independently of the churches.

Out of all these existing tendencies arises the revolutionary principle of giving partial sovereignty to nationalities on a *non-geographical* basis.

Territory as a basis for national sovereign states over which central governments rule was only possible for great nations with a compact and unified nationality. The rapid collapse of the 1919 system proves the impossibility of organizing smaller nations in independent states on a territorial basis where nationalities intermingle. The corrective of minority legislation proved to be a complete bankruptcy.

The part of the world in which a new form of union is a categoric necessity and must be attempted is that part of Europe which lies between Germany and Russia, the Baltic and the Mediterranean. In this part of Europe, whence most of the causes of wars emerge and where some twenty nations are living in such an interpenetrative form that no national frontier can possibly be drawn between them, the formation of states based on nationality is an absolute impossibility.

The only solution acceptable to all nationalities involved seems to be the formation of independent national governments in Warsaw, Prague, Budapest, Belgrade and all the other capitals, governments which should not have power and authority over a certain limited territory, but over a certain nationality, independent of the territory in which they are living. Naturally, the sovereign rights in financial, military and foreign affairs would have to be handled by a federal government selected by them. But in any cultural and national matter, a Rumanian, a Serb and a Hungarian living in the same village should be in a position to follow the Rumanian, Serb and Hungarian national governments.

An analogy to this solution can be found in the religious wars when countries with various religions fought wars against each other until a superior power made it possible for Catholics, Protestants, Mohammedans, Orthodox Greeks, Baptists, Jews, and all others to follow the rules of their own churches without being obliged to kill each other for that reason.

Another important part of the world where the formation of national sovereignties on a non-geographical basis might be the solution of centuries-old struggles is India.

The governments of the various conflicting nations which are fighting for prestige, power, national independence, equilibrium and many other illusions, seem to forget that, besides all this, men also want to eat. So, after a fabulous evolution of industrial production, more millions of people today suffer hunger and misery than ever before.

Nazism and Fascism are merely symptoms of a world crisis and the decadence of a certain system which has nothing any more to do with present conditions. If we want to continue with mass production and dividing this tiny world into a hundred water-tight compartments, if we want to go on being "independent," "sovereign," "neutral," and what not, we shall have wars and wars and wars.

If we believe that "democracy" is the system we *had* in

the past and if we want to go on believing in the same obsolete conceptions, which were merely the expressions of the first attempt of a democratic order established on the basis of eighteenth-century realities, then such a democracy will be smashed like a rotten tree by a tempest.

Democracy is not and can never be a closed rigid system. This is its death. Any closed rigid system must lead to wars, revolutions and dictatorships. Democracy needs constant readjustment. Its institutions require ceaseless rejuvenation. Democracy, therefore, cannot be defined by any system of institutions, existing or to be created.

Democracy is an atmosphere, the only atmosphere in which modern man can live, prosper and progress.

The political organization which is required to solve the problems of war and peace, of freedom and slavery, is not a distant, remote aim, but an immediate necessity. We cannot waste much time. The foundation must be laid now, during this war.

In fact, the establishment of a democratic world order is nothing but the very beginning of the real work we have to do: the solution of the social problems, the problems of production, distribution and consumption, the problem of the general rise in the standard of living for the human race.

Only if we keep in mind these vast social and economic problems can we see the political task before us in its real perspective; that might give us the courage to tackle it without delay and to solve it now.

If we cannot take the resolution to construct now the only possible political framework of our time, we shall have no chance to solve any one of those problems which in fact are the real daily problems of every man and woman, and which should be the principal task of all the governments of our time.

WILDER COLLEGE LIBRARY